WHAT'S *YOUR* LANE?

Career clarity for moms who want to work

a little, a lot, or not at all

Brenda Frances Abdilla

Contains The Division Of Labor Assessment

This book is dedicated to my mother, Lilly Abdilla.
While her mothering was cut short,
the impact of her love is timeless.

WHAT'S *YOUR* LANE?

CAREER CLARITY FOR MOMS WHO WANT TO WORK

A LITTLE, A LOT, OR NOT AT ALL

TABLE OF CONTENTS

INTRODUCTION

How would your life be different if you felt great about your financial contribution to your household *and* your job of raising your kids? What if you
felt fully comfortable with your career status be it stay home, part-time,
full-time? Can you imagine even being energized about it? What if you
and your spouse were on the same page with regard to work, money and
domestic life as well?

   If these seem like trick questions, they're not. It is completely possible
to have a work and home life (a lane) that works for you and your crew
whether your ideal involves staying home full-time, working full-time,
quitting work to pursue a degree or creative project, or asking your spouse
to stay home with the kids so that you can finally hit the gas pedal on your
career. Maybe you just want five minutes free of exhaustion and the growing irritation you feel so that you can think about it and find out what you
really *do want* from a career standpoint. The fact is *the situation you long
for is entirely possible even if it seems unimaginable*. Behind your overwhelm
and mild feelings of tender, loving bitterness are some important keys to
what you *really* want and how you might get it. This book is about helping
you get the answers you need so that you can discover you are already in
the right lane, learn ways to tweak your current set-up to work better for
everyone, or perhaps even change lanes entirely.

   If you are like most mothers, you made your decisions about parenting,
work and schedule mindfully and with the purest of intentions for your
family. Yet, there is also a good chance that you simultaneously trapped

yourself in the process. Initially the set-up that seemed so clear and right for you really worked and felt like the right thing. But somewhere along the way things got messy and complicated and stuff happened. Somehow the key elements changed and like most moms you feel a little mystified about how things got so off track at home and wonder how much longer you can continue this way–and what toll it will take on you.

The Current Reality For Moms:

> ▶ Many mothers feel as though life is happening *to them*. They re-call a time when they had a plan, but it all seems fuzzy now and it's stressful to even think about.

> ▶ Most moms feel stuck with their current circumstances career-wise and secretly wish they had chosen differently when they had the chance.

> ▶ Many mothers, armed with the best of intentions, often pick the "wrong" career lane and try to overcome their personal "wir-ing" by pushing themselves harder and harder to stay with their current choice.

> ▶ Some moms are actually in the "right" career lane for them but don't know it because they are plagued with guilt about their choice.

> ▶ Many moms unintentionally lie to each other about the ups and downs of their particular career lane because they have trouble admitting how hard their life is sometimes. This causes many moms to suffer in silence and not admit they are unhappy until they crack.

Hopefully it's helpful to know that we all screw ourselves in one way or another when it comes to our set-up at home and our careers. We _all_ do it! But motherhood is messy and wonderful and worth it. And in the world of coaching, which is what I do for a living, *why* you screwed yourself is not nearly as important as where you want to go next. In *What's Your Lane?* we will focus on what you want for yourself and your family and how you can go about getting it. What most of us want is something we coaches call *clarity of direction*. When you have a clear sense of where you want to go and why that destination is important to you, it's a lot easier to overcome the obstacles that are part of getting there. Once clarity is part of the pic-ture, everything seems easier, because it *is* easier.

The New Credo For Moms

1. You can be satisfied with your career choice whether you work a little, a lot, or not at all. *And being satisfied is more important than you think.*

2. You do not have to wait until your kids are teenagers or college bound to feel a solid sense of direction and clarity about your level of work (or non-paid work).

3. Trading your mental and physical health for your family is unnecessary and ultimately defeats the entire purpose.

4. Life is a lot easier if you don't hate your spouse. This "state of like" can be achieved much easier when *you* are not doing *everything* at home. This is still true even if he travels, has a highly demanding job, is cutting an album, is under tremendous pressure, works out of state, works like a dog, works for his dad, works two jobs, or rules a small nation.

5. You deserve the real truth about each option so you can make choices based on real information — not outdated parenting conventions that are well-intentioned (sometimes) but do not apply to you.

6. The life that you dream of might actually be within your reach, but you might not know it because you are too stressed, guilty or exhausted to figure out a plan. You deserve a shot at the life of your dreams now, not twenty years from now.

Why I Wrote *What's Your Lane?*

It's lucky for me that I get to spend most of my days as a business and executive coach helping people scrape off the corrosion of stress and overwhelm from their lives so that they can think clearly and move their careers forward. My work both as an executive coach, and for a long time as a recruiter, means I spend a lot of time actively listening and then strategizing with people about career choices. More often than not, family life is at the center of their confusion and stress and at the heart of their greatest desires for something good and solid and workable. Nothing excites me more than working with a person who thinks they are stuck and that their life is a convoluted mess. Often, when clients have a breakthrough moment, they give me credit, but the truth is that the wisdom was there all along, trapped inside and muted by all of the outer noise in their lives. Just talking about coaching people, especially people with kids, makes me atwitter with excitement. I get to spend my days helping people get clear, and once clarity arrives at the party, moving forward becomes remarkably easy.

But I was not always the "Queen of Clarity." When I got pregnant in the late 90's, I was at the top of my own career game. I had two books on the market, and I had just closed the biggest consulting deal of my career. What seemed like five solid years of uphill striving in my business now turned into a high-demand, worldwide professional speaking company. My husband was ecstatic about becoming a father and promised to be an equal player in our new family set-up. Suffice it to say "we had a plan."

Then, in the blink of an eye, we had a newborn and had to move across the country for my husband's dream job. His new job demanded that he consistently work six, twelve hour days a week — every week. I was madly in love with our son and felt lucky beyond words that I had such a beautiful boy. By some kind of magic, I convinced my clients to let me significantly cut my travel and consult virtually so I was running my business from our home. I hired a nanny and was devoted to being the perfect, perfect mom with the highest imaginable standards. Because we had moved away from family it meant that any support we had was on the payroll so we had a big overhead and a big life. Add to this the fact that I suffered from a touch of seasonal mood disorder (we lived in Oregon at the time) and was still struggling with the after-effects of gaining seventy-six pounds during my pregnancy. When I say "after-effects" I mean that I still had not lost the weight and was still fat. Just ponder *that* kind of weight gain for a moment. Seventy-six pounds is like carrying a Spice Girl on your back all day. Suffice it to say, being clear on my life direction was not even remotely a description of me back then.

As I looked around, I realized I was not alone. Motherhood was so empowering and healing and blissful for me and yet it was also intense and exhausting and confusing. It's like a beautiful/dirty little secret. Becoming a mother is fulfilling and delicious in a way that is beyond words, but becoming a mother is also like a sledge hammer to the mom's identity. It seems every mother experiences the private questioning of who she is now and how she will cope and what will become of her after becoming a mother. I thought that because I was a little older and really wanted to be a mom that I would be the exception to the rule—but I was no exception.

In order to cope with my identity crisis, I turned to the professionals for advice and found even more confusion about what the best set-up was when it came to family, parenting, work and the ever illusive "life balance." I have a clear recollection of one book advising me to organize my life and get my kid on a schedule. The author said I should put my baby in front of an open freezer to wake him up for his scheduled feeding and another reminded me that God let his son cry on the cross and so I should let my baby cry (not kidding here—it was a bestseller!). Most of the pregnancy books did not even mention work, or going back to work, except to subtly imply not to do it. Then a whole host of books came out basically telling me to shut up and surrender to motherhood. I had surrendered to motherhood, and it was the best thing ever, but I still had a business to run and was doing everything at home and felt frumpy and tired to the core of my being. It baffled me that my husband's life seemed unchanged (except he wasn't getting much sex anymore). After long days juggling work and baby, my husband would walk through the door at 8:30 p.m., and I would feel indifference for the stranger I had let him become in my mind. I was deeply, profoundly interested in knowing why I should not strangle my lovely husband in his sleep.

What I realized during that time is that whether we are willing to admit it or not, our work *is* tied-up with our identity and how we feel about ourselves once we become mothers. Even if we choose to never, ever work outside the home again, our comfort and confidence with *that* choice impacts our stress level and our outlook on life dramatically. Think about it; we all know one or two moms who are wealthy and have the luxury of staying home with their kids but still have low self-confidence. *Feeling good about our choices cannot be faked or manufactured or even handed down through generations.* Yet, feeling good about ourselves and our career choices is possibly the most important aspect of surviving the long marathon of raising kids. It pains me that we all have to suffer the same collisions as we become mothers.

I wrote this book because it does not have to be that hard. In the same way that we learn that certain diets and eating plans will work like magic for some of us but not all of us—choosing a career lane and a set-up at home has be specific to our needs, values and resources. Also, once we become mothers, the stress of working or not working is inescapably tied to our ability to negotiate duties at home. Why does no one tell us this? Instead, we take on everything in our homes and we end up resenting it. Plus, the current solutions we hear for career and home do not always fit our particular situation. For example, everyone tells us working part-time is the "best of both worlds." If that were true, we would all be working part-time and the conversation would be over. Yet millions of moms who work part-time will tell you that it is great but there are downsides: more work crammed into less time, less money, crusty looks from jealous co-workers and a feeling of never completing anything properly in *any* one category in their lives. We need to hit the pause button on all of the advice and noise coming at us to consider *our* life's particular complexities. This book creates a framework designed for you to get the clarity you need about YOU and *then* you can decide what is best for you and your family.

Is Your Current Lane Working For You?

One way to know if you're currently in the "right" lane is by taking your current set-up at home, work etc. and fast forward five or seven years. Imagine how things might look if nothing significant changed. If you have a sustainable situation you might look ahead and see something that works.

Sure a little more sleep, exercise and money would be great, but you have a sense that you could continue in that direction for quite some time.

On the other hand, you might take your current situation, fast forward five years and think, "Oh, God! NO! There's no way I could keep doing this without a miracle, some drugs or a live-in maid." If you see exhaustion, chaos or insanity in your look-ahead imagination then you might want to consider some other options — *even if you think you have none*. Regardless of how trapped or stuck you may feel in your current lane, if you do not have a sustainable situation then the cost of staying put could far outweigh the cost of making some changes. Before you consider your situation, however, let's look at some examples.

Anna:

Anna is a nurse and has three school age kids. She always quips that if her husband ever got "a real job" she would quit work in a heartbeat. (He's a school teacher). While Anna claims to dream of being a stay home mom, if you look closer you will see that she loves her work and is a very passionate mother as well. She is an extremely competent nurse, a leader in her field, and the doctors she works with both respect and fear her. If you have a sick relative in the hospital, you want Anna on the case. Anna is present for her kids, is intensely interested in them, and she shows up for as many school events as she can.

Not a lot of cooking happens in her home, and sometimes the kids' birthday parties happen months after the event has passed (but it's usually worth the wait). Yet her lane works for her. Even if she won the lottery, there is an excellent chance that she would choose to continue her nursing career. If she flips ahead with her current life by five years or so, things actually look easier as her kids get older and she gets more seniority at work. While nothing is *easy* about Anna's life, she has a lane that works for her personal level of intensity and passion for running a tight ship. Anna would feel so much better in her day-to- day if she enjoyed her lane and looked at what works instead of what does not. Also, Anna might not be as likely to choose staying home, or even working part-time, if she looked at the *reality* of those lanes as it applies to her life instead of just wishing things were different in her lane.

Marin

Marin is a working mom with a different story. She works full-time for an oil company and has excellent pay and benefits. She and her husband have two kids. It took Marin three years to get pregnant the first time. It was a long haul with in-vitro fertilization, several miscarriages, and a heart breaking adoption that failed on the day they were to get the baby. Marin's dream is to be home with them full-time now that she has two healthy children but her husband is adamant that she keep her job because they need the pay and the benefits. He's a great dad, very helpful and committed to his family, and he feels *strongly* that they both should continue to work full-time.

Marin cries a lot. She finds it agonizing to drop her kids off at childcare, and she counts the hours until she can pick them up again. She has grown to hate her job and is starting to resent her husband although she understands his position and his reasoning about work. When Marin imagines her situation in five years, she becomes depressed and sad. She does not think her marriage will last, and she sees overindulged children because their mom feels guilty being away from them all day. Marin does not have a sustainable situation at home or work. The truth is, however, Marin is not as trapped as she may think. And simply quitting her job will not magically make everything better either. First of all she understandably has some healing and grief work to do before she makes any big decisions and she and her husband must learn to communicate more effectively with each other. If Marin can figure out some things about the fears and the values driving her desires then she can discover what she values the most and move in that direction from a position of clarity — not stress and sadness. With some time spent exploring Marin might see that she has a variety of options at her disposal and that life does not have to be such a struggle.

How This Book Works:

You may relate to Anna or Marin or you may have a very different story. Whatever the case, you will come away from this book knowing what career lanes appeal to you, which don't and how your home set-up limits or supports you. When we talk about your career, always imagine it holding hands with your life set-up because the two are co-dependent. (When I refer to life "set-up" I am talking about the division of labor in your home, the dynamic between you and your spouse and the overall approach to family and parenting in your home). By the time you finish this book you'll know a lot more about what you truly want and how you might plan to get it. With that goal in mind, we will look at where you stand currently and help you figure out what beliefs, values, and important life experiences impact your parenting and career decisions and choices. These things already impact your choices but we need to bring them into the light. Then, I will give you a new framework from which to look at your life and your options. We will look at the issue of whether you want to work and how much, and how it impacts you and your family. I will explain in detail the lane choices that are available to you and the pros and cons of each. In the beginning of the book, I will refer you to some self-assessment tools, which are all found in Chapter Ten to help you build that clarity we talked about earlier. The exercises are part of the process I use in my coaching practice. These exercises will help unearth your beliefs, values, dreams, doubts and fears and help you see how they affect your choices. You'll also learn some concrete strategies and powerful coping exercises like "Going to the Ugly" and "The Division of Labor Assessment." In the last chapter, we pull it all together and lay the groundwork for you to move forward in a way that reflects *your* most important values and resources as well as your own personal wiring and the current needs of your family.

Just a quick note about the language used in this book (and by language I mean vernacular, not swearing, although a few swear words might have been used to lighten up a point or two).

Spouse

Because there are so many variations on how we define a family and the relationships in it, for the purposes of this book, consider the term "spouse" interchangeable with: husband, wife, life partner, lover, mate, *otha motha*, better half, the guy your kids call "uncle," or the dude.

Work

Also, for ease and speed, when I talk about "work," I'm referring to the kind that earns money. Yes, raising children is absolutely real work, but to keep the reading fast and easy for busy moms, we will refer to "work" as the income-earning kind.

Mothers

With all due respect to men (dads and dudes), for the purposes of this book, mothers are not just parents. They are women. Men have come a long way in their parenting roles, but the stay home/work conflict is not the same for dads. Perhaps this is because men are still "expected" to work, which is wrong and unjust, but that will have to be in someone else's book. This book is about and for women who are moms who are grappling with the questions that we face.

Disclaimer

All of the stories and anecdotes are true but the names and circumstances have been changed to make them unrecognizable. The stories of my own life, however, including those revealing my very own weird personality traits, are told as they happened — even though they may seem fictional, freakish or exaggerated — unfortunately they are not.

Me

For the record, I am not a life balance expert and certainly not a parenting or marriage expert. (Even though my idea of renegotiating chores with my husband over a pitcher of margaritas has been used by others extensively.)

I am a career and business expert who is deeply passionate about mothers and families. Figuring out what we want and asking for it can actually be a bit un-balancing in many of the key areas of your life (at first) but it's worth the effort if you end up in a lane that functions well for your life and family, and you can see yourself thriving in that lane for a long time.

Before You Begin..........

First time coaching clients often think that coaching is all about action steps and accountability. They dutifully show up with blank paper in hand, ready to make the list and overcome procrastination or their lack of motivation and get to work. While good coaching certainly leads to action, it's the thing that happens *between* the coaching and the action that makes all the difference in the world. You can call it the process, the space, alteration, deep change or inner clarity or a shift....but that shift is what this book is all about. Here you can contemplate your life and choices through the lives of other moms and through some very frank discussion about your options. Perhaps you will get some little or BIG ideas and epiphanies. You may finish the book fast and tweak a few things right away that make a big impact in your life. Perhaps you will begin to feel less resigned to a particular lane or situation. Great! Or maybe you will think of a way to approach your current boss and ask for what you want. My hope is that this book will be the place you can be honest about your current set-up and trust that you will figure some things out. Trust your mind and your process and allow yourself to answer questions honestly and know you will not be judged. Thank you for letting me help you with one of, if not *the*, most important aspects of your life as a mother.

In the long run, we shape our lives, and we shape ourselves.
The process never ends until we die. And the choices we make
are ultimately our own responsibility.

-Eleanor Roosevelt

COACHING ASSIGNMENT #1   **TIME: 10 MINUTES**

Read page *99*: *The Power Of A Question*

Then turn to page 101 and complete the Beginning Assessment-
Where am I now?

PART I:

THE ROAD TO CLARITY

CHAPTER ONE

CHECKING UNDER THE HOOD

What's *Really* Driving Your Decisions?

In the month of my seventeenth birthday, my mother died after a seven year battle with breast cancer. Nine short months later, my father died suddenly of a heart attack. My parents had immigrated to the US from Malta in 1951 to give their children a better life. They became hardworking, patriotic American citizens who were completely devoted to their seven children. My mom stayed home with us while my dad worked in the factory at Ford Motor Company and managed to make ends meet. If you had met my parents you would describe them as adorable and find their accents and food fascinating. Somehow, some way my siblings and I survived this tragedy and have all gone on to lead productive, full lives. My traditional upbringing and the early loss had a huge impact on my life decisions and my parenting decisions later, but it was a long time before I realized that my experiences were dominating my parenting decisions without my awareness.

I have always considered myself a feminist—a champion of women and women's rights. In my earlier years, one might have used the word "feminazi" (or perhaps crazy, over-the-top-man hater). Somewhere in my head, I had connected my mother's selfless devotion to her husband and children to her early and untimely death. On the good side of this erroneous belief was the drive it created for me in my career and my passion for empowering women. But on the other side, I have been, on occasion, a fairly defensive pain in the rear when it comes to my perceptions of unfair or unequal treatment of women. I used to feel plagued with guilt as I recalled my mother serving us meals, like a waitress, in her own home. A few years ago, I had a vivid dream that my mom looked directly into my eyes and then gently stroked my face, and said, "I liked it you know. I didn't mind." It was as if my mom was coming from the beyond to say, "For God's sake, give it a rest, girl!" I have since relaxed a bit on feminism and the choices people make. And come to think of it, I often serve my family and our guests, and I do it with a lot of pleasure.

The more powerful, silent decision-maker in my life, however, was the early loss. I learned that, in a flash, life can change and knock you down hard. To this day, if the phone rings very late or very early I feel stricken with fear. The night before our wedding, I made my husband, Kevin, promise me that he would never die on me, that even if he was so mangled he wished he were dead, he would fight to live because he promised he would. And he promised. Remarkably, he still showed up for our wedding the next day. When our son was born a few years later, I felt completely overcome by love and the desire to protect him. However, other people in my life say I was like a rabid dog baring my teeth at anyone who came near us. —tomato, *tomato*. Okay, so I might have been a tad overprotective. Our Portland nanny still makes fun of the "safety rules" I had back then.

So what's wrong when a person doesn't want their precious family to die and makes lots of rules about avoiding danger and keeping them safe? Well, a lot! The problem is that there is no peace when we make decisions from a place of fear. Can you ever really be safe enough? Sure enough? Careful enough? The answer is no. And we know this on some level. *We know that if we let the fear of what could happen dominate our decisions, we achieve only one thing – more fear.* Frankly, I drove everyone crazy back then and my imagination made me crazy too. Eventually I had to learn that I cannot control the world; I can only control *some* things and that list of things in my span of control is very, very short. I am still a safety mom, but now, with each and every parenting decision, I check myself to make sure I am making the decision out of a sane place inside and not the fearful, worry wart that lives within me as well.

Now It's Your Turn

When we make decisions about life—especially about our families—we bring with us our very own, unique bag of beliefs and fears, hopes and impactful experiences. This can range from wanting to attend every sporting event your child plays, because your mother never attended yours, to wanting to stay home with your kids because your mother did so in such a beautiful and positive way. You may also notice that your partner comes with his or her own bag of tricks, as do your in-laws, your parents, your neighbors, your political party—you get the point. It's time to become aware of what is in these bags, and then you get to decide if it's an important part of your decision making process in the future. Your life experiences and probably your fears are making some big decisions for you right now whether you know it or not. Now is your chance to just take a peek and see what's running you. In my case, everyone else in my life knew that I was operating from an intense fear of loss. But I didn't! I thought I was being a perfectly natural new mom and that every mom felt seized with panic at the thought of letting someone else hold her baby.

Keep in mind that you don't have to change a thing about your current situation as you explore this aspect of your life. Knowing what is behind your decisions can be extremely insightful and has value simply in the knowing. In my experience, there are four areas where you can discover the origin of most of your central parenting decisions.

The Four Elements That Impact Our Parenting (And Related Career) Decisions:

1. Impactful Life Experiences

2. Our Silent Judgment Of Others

3. Our Secret Anger, Upset And Resentment

4. The Division Of Labor In Our Home

1. Impactful Life Experiences

What life experience powered your big decisions?

Christy and Bob have three kids. Christy is a police officer and worked her first five years in the Special Victims Unit. Bob runs a company that does bookkeeping for small businesses. Bob and Christy agreed even before having their first child that they would never, ever use a babysitter for their children. Christy's work experience in the SVU gave her an inventory of all of the horrible crimes that humans can perpetrate on one another. Of course the horror of the images she'd seen became more upsetting once she had children of her own. Plus, Bob's younger sister had been molested by an uncle when they were children so he gave Christy no argument when she suggested that they alter their schedules to make sure that one of them was always with the children. Christy worked afternoons and would get home at midnight and Bob worked days. Bob and Christy's powerful life experiences told them their children were not safe with others.

It's okay to have deep and meaningful reasons for your choices

Martin and Heather have four kids. In the 1950's, Martin's parents escaped from the Ukraine with him and his older sister. Martin's family lived a hardworking and poor existence in upstate New York. His parents reminded him daily that they risked their lives to give their children a life of freedom and opportunity. Martin studied and worked hard and earned a full scholarship to an Ivy League college. He was quickly climbing his way up the corporate ladder when he met Heather while she was visiting New York, and they fell in love.

Heather had an idyllic upbringing on her family's farm in North Dakota. Her first memories as a child were pretending she was the momma of many children. Heather moved to New York, and after their first child was born, the couple decided that she would stay home with the children and he would devote himself to a career that would provide them with the resources and support they needed. Martin's finance career ambitions moved the young family to Germany, Japan, England and Norway in the first six years of marriage and eventually landed them back in New York where they bought a small farm and had three more kids. Martin and Heather's life experiences had a big impact on their desire to create what they saw as an idyllic upbringing for their children.

Both couples made their decisions based on life experiences, as we ALL do. Both couples experienced victories and difficulties based on their choices, as we all do. About five years into their plan, Christy and Bob soon realized that their tag-team parenting left them both constantly exhausted and they almost never had time together as a complete family. They decided this plan was not working for them and that the trade-off was too extreme. Bob cut back his client load for a few years so they could get more family time and when their youngest reached age ten, the couple decided that it was okay to hire some outside help to fill in the gaps when Bob went back to a full-time client load. Christy went back to the day shift so they had most evenings together as a family. Had they not made those adjustments, despite their powerful fears and beliefs, their marriage might not have lasted or their exhaustion may have taken its toll.

For the other couple, Martin and Heather, keeping the core plan dominated their decisions, and that worked out as well. Martin and Heather remained committed to their choice to have Heather stay home even when tough economic times forced them to sell the family farm and move into a smaller home. Now that the kids are all grown and the youngest is in college, Heather is working on a documentary film about the healing power of flower herbs.

Now it's time for you to explore your beliefs and what life experiences helped to shape those beliefs. Think about the parenting beliefs that you feel strongly about and see if you can trace them to an experience. Perhaps you do not believe in hitting your children and can trace it back to the violent upbringing you had, or maybe you drive your kids to school because you had to walk in the cold weather (uphill both ways). You are just taking inventory here so there is no need to change anything.

He who knows others is wise; he who knows himself is enlightened.

— Lao Tzu

COACHING ASSIGNMENT #2   **TIME: 10 MINUTES**
Turn to page 103 and complete the *Parenting Beliefs* exercise

2. Our Silent (And Not-So-Silent) Judgment Of Others

What are your favorite gripes about other mothers?

Do you ever look around and see a whole lot of terrible, misguided parenting? Like seeing a mom with her pre-teen child talking on an iPhone or a mother completely tuned out to her kid's loud and obnoxious attempts to get her attention? As funny as it seems, what you notice the most about other mothers (both positive and negative) can give you a big clue about your own hidden beliefs. It can seem like there is no end to crappy parenting happening around us, but when we silently judge other moms, two things are going on: the first is that we are attempting to clarify our own beliefs by noticing the mother who appears to have a different belief or value than we do. This is also true when we affirm another mother's actions — we are essentially affirming ourselves. Both positive or negative judging are an effective, yet slightly twisted, way of knowing what we like and don't like.

The second thing going on when we judge is that our reaction to the situation is actually telling us something about our overall stress level and satisfaction with our current "program." *If we look closely at what we are judging, it is clear that we are the most judgmental when we are stressed out about our own lives or just really tired and exhausted by life.* Think about it: when you are in a really good place with your own life, you're fairly unaffected by another mother's parenting choices (not counting abuse, of course). Conversely, when the behavior or choices of another mom create that visceral, powerful "wrongness" reaction inside, you can bet it has more to do with you than her.

In the past, my particular hot button was parents who traveled on airplanes with infants on their laps. I believed the practice was unsafe, selfish and downright reckless. My justification for the judgment was that I had traveled nearly a million miles in the 1990s and had plenty of stories about unexpected turbulence. But my experience was in no way a proportioned response to justify the rabid judgments I developed about parents traveling with lap-children. I am embarrassed to admit that I used to tell to my family members with children (as well as a few people I didn't even know) that if they could not afford a seat for their baby then they should not be traveling. In retrospect, I can now see that was just my belief that I had to control as much of the world as I could to protect *my* family. It was my fear of loss rearing up again. My calmer current self knows that people have to make choices, that there is actually very little likelihood that an infant will be harmed in flight (certainly less chance than in an automobile), and that ultimately it's none of my damn business. Now when I look at a baby on a mom's lap, I feel nothing but warm and fuzzy about the family and secretly hope that I might get to hold the baby (and of course that the baby does not cry the whole way).

How sure are you about what you see?

The weird thing about judging others is that you're probably wrong anyway. In most cases when we judge others, we do so with a whole bucket-load of assumptions. Like maybe the pre-teen on the iPhone is chatting with her dad in Afghanistan, or perhaps she's a tech genius and invented the application she is using currently. Who knows? Most of us are seeing others through the lens of our own life experience and are judging without the pesky undertaking of checking our facts or even knowing what the hell we are actually looking at.

Author and life balance expert, Mary LoVerde, calls this habit "filling in the blanks." In her book *I Used to Have a Handle on Life but It Broke*, she writes, "Do you sometimes live in 'The World According to Me?' This is a world in which you gather some of the data, then fill in the blanks (often erroneously) with your interpretation- and declare that your conclusion must be true."

When you find yourself judging, make a mental note to ask yourself what you might *not* be seeing. You can choose to check in with yourself and see what life experience that judgment might be associated with from your end. You can also notice if you are just exhausted and "hate everyone" right now.

Please don't feel bad if you are guilty of judging and filling in the blanks. I have many stories of filling in the blanks and then later discovering that I was dead wrong. My friend Mary, the author quoted above, had to change my name when putting my stories about filling in the blanks for her book so that her readers would not hate me. If I can learn to quiet my mind and not fill in the blanks, you can too.

> *Don't believe everything you think.*
>
> *— Byron Katie*

COACHING ASSIGNMENT #3   **TIME: 10 MINUTES**
Turn to page 106 and complete the *My Unique Judgments* exercise

3. Our Secret Anger, Upset and Resentment

Got anger?

Do you ever just wake up angry? Or feel suddenly bitter and upset, seemingly out of nowhere? Part of what drives our life decisions and possibly the key to finding the best path *for us* is often locked behind a wall of stress and exhaustion. Perhaps you are feeling a low-grade kind of anger right now, and maybe you have resigned yourself to feeling a mix of exhaustion, resentment and crankiness, accepting this as the "new you." Perhaps you have some issues that you filed away in one of the airtight "Tupperware containers" you keep inside of yourself. You know, the one you try to ignore until it bursts from the pressure inside of you, astonishing loved ones and innocent bystanders?

What if your anger, exhaustion and even the bitterness were actually a gift? A nudge from your subconscious that there is a better way or an important aspect or angle you missed? Unless you are always a bitter, negative person, then feeling awful can be an indicator that the object of your agony is worth exploring further. Yes, this is worth exploring even if you think nothing can be done in your situation—even if you think you are completely stuck and feel that you've already made your choices. Even if you just *know* your husband will never change. Even then. Even *you*.

The gift of your emotions

Psychologists tell us that there's no such thing as a bad or wrong emotion. In my work with clients, I see strong emotions as valuable gifts when they appear—especially the negative and unexpected ones. Bitterness, anger and feelings of perpetual dissatisfaction are gifts when you teach yourself to unwrap them and find the prize inside. Of course we are conditioned not to "go there." It's perfectly natural to think that exploring the negative emotion will make things worse. I can assure you that 100% of my clients are reluctant to proceed when an awful, stomach-churning feeling comes up. We are conditioned to suck it up and put a positive spin on it immediately. Ironically, when we ignore or try to repress our emotions, we tend to make decisions *from* that place. Acknowledging and discovering what is behind some of our most powerful emotions is very different from making a big decision based upon them. Making a decision from a place of anger, resentment or even fatigue is a bad idea all around. It's better to set up a system for yourself to "court" the negative emotion a bit and see what else you discover. There are many ways to find the gift behind negative emotions--I use a method I call *Going to the Ugly* (which you can try first hand next). *GTTU* is a strategy you can apply to each and every gripe you have (and one that might keep you off of the next episode of *Snapped*.)

Going to the Ugly encourages you to admit the less-than-hopeful thoughts you are having about your life right now or about a currently frustrating situation. I use this exercise with my business-coaching clients and it's a favorite because it's both useful and therapeutic. Once you do it a few times, your mind will automatically use it with other issues that come up and you will get efficient at the practice. There is an example and a form to use in Chapter Ten, but in the meantime, think about the area of your life you are most frustrated with, the one where you feel the most stuck, and ponder what else might really be going on. Resist the temptation to put a positive spin on it. Remember there are no wrong or bad emotions. Let yourself feel whatever you are feeling and see if one perfectly acceptable emotion actually leads to other more surprising ones.

> *Bitch is the new black.*
>
> *-Tina Fey/SNL*

Do you need a mental health professional? If you are having thoughts of harming yourself or others get yourself the help you need. Seriously, this exercise is not a substitute for therapy or for working with a licensed mental health professional.

COACHING ASSIGNMENT #4   **TIME: 20 MINUTES**
Turn to page 109 and complete *The Going to the Ugly* exercise

4. The Division Of Labor In Your Home

What's fair?

Our set-up at home impacts our choices and decisions about career more than any other. Sometimes the division of labor and handling of life at home is very specifically agreed upon, and other times it evolves from situations we thought were temporary but became permanent. Perhaps you had a period of unemployment and decided to pick up the slack at home and now seven years later you are back to work but still carrying the same load. Or maybe right after your second baby your spouse started traveling full-time, and you got into the habit of doing nearly everything at home, but now it seems like you would be whining if you brought up the inequity after so much time has passed. Maybe your husband does a lot but somehow you both seem to be tired all the time, and there is an endless list of stuff that does not get done. It can feel overwhelming just to think about all that has to be accomplished.

Our math is jacked

Consider the following from a logical perspective: If you are a mom of two kids and working part-time with a spouse who earns eighty percent of the income, should you, in turn, do eighty percent of the housework and family management? What if you have just one kid? Should that equation change? Should you get a full-time job? What if you have five kids and earn 25% of the household income? What if you earn 70% but have three kids? The math will never, ever work if you try to figure it out from a logical, fair and square perspective. Not only will life feel unfair for both you *and your spouse* but staying married and sane may become increasingly difficult—assuming that is the goal. You have to refigure this entire equation by adding in the illusive *missing variable*.

My son was about four years old when I had a groundbreaking, sky opening revelation. I felt like shouting it in the streets. The revelation was the answer to why I was so frustrated and why I was frustrating the heck out of my poor husband. It felt like *he* had it so easy and that I was burdened with the weight of the world. Worse, I felt like a failure in about thirteen categories, and he would often ask me with exasperation what more I wanted from him. What I wanted was relief! As I looked around, all my girlfriends felt the same with varying degrees of frustration or resignation *regardless of their career choices* and set-up. Nobody had a life I wanted and nobody had it "figured out."

The missing variable

The revelation was this: *our life is an <u>entity</u> in and of itself.* I am not talking about our homes, which of course require huge time investment. I am talking about our LIVES once kids come into the picture. Of course, on the surface we are all aware of this before we have kids. We knew that kids needed care and feeding and supplies and attention and organizing and the juggling related to their presence. We prepare for the structure their lives will require, and our support system helps us anticipate that aspect of parenting. We all know that we have roles in life and that they may or may not include work outside the home and that the grass will still need to be cut, etc. And we all know that we have to care for our primary relationship and take steps to preserve and protect it. Yes, affirmative, we all know that. We know that we should invest in and nurture our extended family, stay in touch and make holidays special to create positive rituals and carry on family tradition, etc. Of course. Got it. But that does not even begin to explain the effort, attention and level of involvement it takes to *make a life*, keep a home, and raise a family. The missing variables in our equation are all of the items that get done in addition to everything else but never make the to-do list.

Random examples of the *missing variable*:

▶ Burying the pet salamander who lost his battle with the family cat this morning (gratefully it happened in the yard and not in the living room). The burial is scheduled right after consoling your wailing children who are waking the neighbors on a school day and on the same morning you have been without food (OR COFFEE) because you are scheduled for a fasting blood test at the doctor's office.

▶ Answering the question, "Should I text Jason again?" Your fifteen-year-old daughter, who has been dumped by her summer boyfriend on the first day of tenth grade, needs an answer NOW.

▶ Responding to the fourth citation you have received this month from the Homeowner's Association stating that you are in violation of the rules with your kiddie-pool set-up (which you know you are in complete compliance).

▶ Figuring out quickly if you should call poison control or animal control because your toddler just ate goose poop.

▶ Lice. Need I say more?

Those seen and unseen elements of a *life* are an entity in and of themselves. Moms tend to take on this entire, massive category without being completely aware of just how much extra work it entails. People without children call it "momma drama." Individually each item seems too silly to even mention but the accumulation of urgent and important items we simply *handle* can build up resentment and frustration and make us feel crazy. Later, as we take a look at the division of labor in your life, keep this missing variable concept in mind.

Is simply *simplifying* THE answer?

Anyone who says, "Well, our mothers worked it out and they had fifteen kids at home!" can bite me. Today's world *is* different than former generations in important *and* relevant ways. A home, an extended family, a social life, school, neighbors, obligations to the world outside of work—all of these things together are dramatically different from other generations. Sure, we could all cut back a bit and do less and say yes to less. Absolutely! You can simplify all day long, but if you have kids in the house, life is just more complicated.

Probably fifteen of the twenty things you did today did not even exist in 1950. Think about it. Just take any one of a hundred categories—safety, for example—and consider the processes and steps that are now required to address it with even the lowest standard of parenting. Do we really want to go back to having toddlers standing in the front seat while we are driving seventy-five miles an hour? If the answer is, "of course not," then car seats are required. And car seats come with car seat research, requirements, best practices, recalls, price comparison and, of course, installation in one or more cars. And car seats are one, tiny item in the safety category that previous generations did not have to deal with. Add to that stroller safety, crib safety, infant death rates, vaccination reactions, food allergies, super germs and cyber-bullying just to name a few. Your parents or your grandparents raised their kids blissfully unaware of these issues. For today's parents, this is barely breaking the surface on the list of hundreds of safety issues that are current hot topics.

Now think about communication. When you have children, the people in your life and extended family want to know about them and might want to communicate with them. In the 1950s, my parents emigrated from the island of Malta. To communicate with the extended family they left behind, they wrote letters a few times a year. The distance and the long delivery time meant that there was very little expectation of staying in close touch with their families. In contrast, today's parents have family stretched all over the globe, and while the methods of communication have improved significantly, they have also raised the bar for staying connected. We're expected to keep in touch in real-time through a variety of channels: phone, Facebook, Twitter, family website or blog, SKYPE, text messaging, voicemail, instant messaging—oh, and let's not forget to upload some fresh photos to Great Grandma's digital picture frame at the nursing home. The ability to stay constantly connected is wonderful and a true gift from technology AND it creates the expectation that we do so. I will give you one guess who handles most of the to-dos related to the communication category in most households. Mom, of course. And, will monitoring and managing family communications to the outside world ever make the list of acknowledged items? Probably not. It just gets done.

I am not saying that previous generations did not have their share of difficulty and challenge. Of course they did. But comparison is simply not fair. Sure we have more resources than other generations did, but our lives are more complex, and pat answers like "simplify your life" are not helpful. What *is* helpful is to start noticing all of the tasks that we handle and complete in this unaccounted-for category so that we can decide if the tasks are keepers or not or if we are doing too much.

Now do the math

As you think ahead about the next week in your life notice how many of the things that need to get done simply fall in your column by default. There is an assessment for you to complete next but even more important is your awareness of all that goes on and how much of it you take on automatically. The idea with the assessment is to look more closely at all the "to-dos" in our lives and to itemize them accurately with an attempt to include some of the missing variable items in your life. In the future, when dividing up duties, you might think twice before saying, "You take care of our income and I will take care of everything else." *That everything else is a lot more than most of us could have ever imagined.* Even if you come from a long line of women who took care of everything else, what it takes to manage a family and a home is a whole different equation by today's standards.

> *You shut your mouth when you're talking to me!*
> *-Rebecca DeMorne, opening scene of*
> *the movie The Wedding Crashers*

COACHING ASSIGNMENT #5   TIME: 20 MINUTES
Turn to page 121 and complete the *Division of Labor In Your Home —Assessment* and related reading

There is no doubt that your pregnancies, birth story, upbringing or life experiences are impacting your decisions today. Now you get to choose if they continue to have an impact going forward.

> *Many hands make light work.*
> *- John Haywood, 1497*

NOTES:

SHIFTING GEARS

I am continually surprised by how deeply rooted and widely accepted the "folklore" about parenting persists in our culture. It took me more than ten years to write this book (okay fifteen), and one of my writing procrastination strategies was to tell myself how much parenting had progressed and that moms would not need my empowering words because they would have it figured out by the time I finished the book. Yet, when I overhear people passing on outdated counsel to moms about money, kids and happiness I am reminded that some concepts, however illogical, die hard.

Here's a good one: **Why have kids in the first place if you are not going to raise them yourself?** This statement makes sense if you are thinking about sending your six-year-old to boarding school or putting your three kids up for adoption or giving serious thought to leaving your four-year-old twins at your mother's house until they go through puberty. But if you are simply considering *childcare* then this adage is complete poppycock. Having someone *watch* your kids does not mean you are letting someone else *raise* them. Please! Our kids spend more time in school than nearly any other place and no one thinks school is "raising" their kid.

The folklore, while universal, widespread and pervasive just does not hold up to even the tiniest bit of logic or further questioning. For example, would having your mother watch your kids on Monday and sending them to a great little day care on Tuesdays and Wednesdays and then you being home all day Thursday through Sunday mean that someone else was "half" raising your kids? Of course not. How about if you work full-time, and you and your favorite co-worker share a fabulous full-time nanny for your babies? Is the nanny raising both of your kids for you? Hardly. But the folklore can have a powerful influence in our decision making process because it pervades in spite of the fact that it makes no sense. Also, some of this stuff is so commonly shared that it can take on a factual quality. Listed below are some of the most popular myths.

Once we strip away the mythology of the less-than-logical pieces of advice, you will have a more accurate framework to use moving forward in your decision-making process. First we tackle a few key myths together, and then you can apply the same logic to the "gems" that your grandma, your childless cousin and people on airplanes who cannot stop themselves from sharing their "wisdom" may spring on you. And please don't feel bad if you have uttered these adages yourself. I certainly did before someone else pointed out that my assertions did not really make much sense.

The Most Pervasive Myths:

-If childcare costs the same as your income, then you should quit work and stay home.

-Your maternal instincts will guide you.

-It would be ideal to find work that you can do while your children nap or attend school.

-Any decision you make is completely justified if you are at your wit's end and can't take it anymore.

-If you are unhappy with your situation, you should change it.

-Your career decisions or professional interests should not upset the flow of things at home.

-You made your choice; now you have to stick with it.

> *A responsible person must learn to unlearn what he has learned.*
> *A responsible person must have the courage to rethink and change*
> *his thoughts. Of course there must be good and sufficient reason for*
> *unlearning what he has learned and for recasting his thoughts.*
> *-Ralph Waldo Emerson*

The *New* Rules Of The Road For Moms:

Myth: If childcare costs the same as your income, then quit and stay home.
New Rule: Don't say it's about the money when it is really about something else.

Money is funny. Maybe it's some ancestral coding, puritanical work ethic or industrial age hand-me-down within each of us that tells us any amount of misery and stress is okay — *as long as it is for the money.* We tie all kinds of decisions to "the money" and let it serve as an end-of-story type of answer. It's the decider, the conversation ender. In reality, money logic does not *always* hold up, and recognizing the real reason behind these decisions could be of great use to you and your partner when you choose your lane or change lanes.

Let's take, for example, the conventional logic, that encourages a mother to stay home with her babies if she currently earns less than or equal to what childcare costs. Take a professional woman making $35,000 per year who becomes pregnant. Her husband makes $125,000 per year. The woman does not love her job, but she likes it well enough. Suppose that during her eighth month of pregnancy she looks into the daycare provider offered through her workplace. (Her delay on this task is a sign of her ambivalence, which is valid and important, but it is hidden by the money argument). The cost of full-time daycare is $800 per month, but she doesn't like the appearance of the place, or maybe even the smell, and the kids there seem lonely to her. She looks into hiring a private nanny and learns the cost is $2,400 per month. She calculates that if she pays the nanny $2,400 per month, and takes into consideration the monthly dry-cleaning, gas and parking costs associated with her job, she will be paying out her full salary in childcare. She talks with her husband, and they agree she should quit her job after the baby is born and stay home.

This sounds perfectly logical, right? No. Sorry. It's not logical if this decision is really based on the money. The couple is not calculating the fact that childcare costs are the highest with an infant and are reduced significantly after age two (when preschools and daycare become more of an option — and with the increased options, she is likely to find one that meets her standards and her budget). Even excluding promotions, with modest salary increases mom may be making $38,000 two years from now — and overall childcare costs could be reduced to $1800 per month, leaving an upside of $16,400. Also, staying employed opens up all kinds of mother-friendly options (part-time, flex-time, consulting, actually finding a job she loves, etc.) that become significantly less likely once she leaves the workplace for an indefinite period. Most importantly, why should they compare the cost of childcare only against *her* income? Why is her career suddenly so expendable? If you calculate the couple's combined earnings, childcare represents only 20% of the total. He is the one with the giant income. Why not calculate childcare against *his* salary, or at least factor it in?

This couple needs to look more closely at their values and their internal conflicts and make their decisions from that standpoint. The above example is just not a "financial decision". There is more at play here. There is no right or wrong lane; maybe she has always wanted to stay home. That is an excellent reason to do so. But basing the decision solely on the amount of her salary compared against childcare is *not* a good argument in their case. And, if her spouse is a logical guy who is a tiny bit nervous about the loss of income on her part, you can bet he will be counting the years until she is ready to go back to work when she may secretly be planning to stay home indefinitely. And that is always a fun ride for a marriage. Whoops.

Myth: Your maternal instincts will guide you.
New Rule: Learn to distinguish between your maternal instincts and your fear.

Anyone who knows me knows that I am a "safety mom." I got this way partly due to my own life experiences and partly due to the fact that when my son was an infant, I became practically addicted to the hard core investigative news shows that were popular on TV in the 90s. I fell asleep each night with visions of sex offenders, identity thieves, kidnappers, abusive parents, scam artists, child pornographers and drug dealers lurking in my mind. I did not realize how much I was internalizing all of the scary news until our son was four months old and my husband got his dream job, and we moved to Portland, Oregon. In Portland, I was suddenly faced with leaving my son in the care of people I did not know while I went to the office each day. I became a walking encyclopedia of bad things that can happen to good people — especially babies. I nearly went insane. My instinctual alarms were going off constantly. I was a Paranoid Paula, an "awfulizer," Debbie Downer. I was a neurotic mess.

I shared a nanny for a time with my only friend in Portland, Kym, who had a baby girl the same age as my son. Like a true girlfriend, I managed to get Kym worked up about all of the things that could happen to our little babies in the care of someone other than us. Somehow I convinced her that good parents worried constantly about their kids and pre-imagined the bad things in order to avoid them. Even though Kym's youngest was her third baby, and she was infinitely saner about parenting than I was, together we got anxious about a long list of potential catastrophes ranging from the nanny forgetting one of our babies at the mall to someone kidnapping the whole group from the children's museum to car accidents with unrestrained children being ejected on the highway. It was the parenting version of plague, locusts and pestilence kind of stuff. One day, while I was asking her how long she thought it would take our nanny, Kristin, to steal our babies and get them to the state border, she suggested that perhaps our "maternal instincts" were not at work here, but instead it was just plain old fear. I thought about that and realized she was right! I was letting my imagination run wild while scaring myself (and others) into frenzy and labeling it maternal instinct.

From that point forward, I taught myself to distinguish between what I was afraid of and what my instincts were really telling me. I learned that my instincts whisper and my fears scream. I learned that my instincts are just a flutter of thought; a hint; a wisp, whereas my fears were dramatic and cinematic and almost always involved bloodshed and crying and a

SWAT team. Once I started questioning the thoughts I was having, the fears got quieter and quieter and the instincts got louder. I was, and continue to be, afraid of a lot of things. But now I try not to make my parenting decisions from a place of fear.

I met another mom a few years ago whose children were age six and eight at the time. She was complaining about feeling exhausted and resentful and distant from her husband. She had not worked since her first child was born, and more importantly, she had never left her kids alone except for school. Not once had this mom allowed her children to attend a birthday party or be watched by a relative or allowed a girlfriend or neighbor to take her kids as an act of reciprocity for the time she had taken theirs. She did not allow her husband to put the kids to bed ever. When I asked her how this was possible, she said, "I was put on this earth to protect my children, and that is what I am doing." The part of me that used to be crippled by fear totally understood what this woman was saying. I got that she wanted to protect her babies. And I got that there is much to be afraid of. Every parent knows that on some level.

The bummer is that *making decisions out of fear will only create more fear*—not peace. Fear feeds on itself and only creates one thing—more fear. The woman I met was a prime example of that. She started out simply trying to protect her kids, and that fear evolved somehow into giving up her entire life and trusting no one. How will that impact her kids? How will they trust and learn? Part of life is admitting that we simply do not have control over everything and everyone—not even our kids.

Our culture encourages mothers to tune into our intuition and do what it tells us. (This is really code for doing what THEY want us to do!) So learning to distinguish between fear and instinct is a subtle but important skill to attain when it comes to parenting and career choice. For example, your instincts may tell you to surprise your nanny or daycare provider by showing up early on occasion just to see what there is to see or randomly check your teenager's computer history and Facebook activity.

Your fear, on the other hand, tells you to buy a "nanny-cam" and plant it in the diaper bag (yes, I saw that on *Hard Copy* in the 1990s). Or to hire a private investigator to follow your college student on campus so you can *really* know what they are up to (I know, great idea, right?). Or your fear may even convince you to scramble to get your teaching certificate so you can actually teach at your kid's middle school to keep them "safe." These are all over-the-top, real life examples that were born from fear, not instinct.

As you make decisions about your career, family, parenting, etc., listen to the voice in your head and see if you can find out if it is fear or instinct talking. There are *many* paths to get what we want, whether it is safety, supreme influence over our children's upbringing, retirement money, food and shelter, equality, etc. Pay attention to what is really going on inside and learn to differentiate between the two perspectives. Acknowledge your fears, but avoid making decisions based on those fears. Over time you will be able to tell the difference.

As for Kristin, the nanny I shared with Kym, she provided us with wonderful childcare and remains an important part of our lives and never once headed for the state border with our infants in tow.

> *You can worry or pray. But not both.*
>
> *- Rapper Fifty-cent*

Myth: It would be ideal to find work that you can do while your children nap or attend school.

New Rule: Beware of easy answers or shortcuts to money and career.

Career choices, finances and childcare are complicated issues. Any plan that promises a cure for what ails all moms in one fell swoop is probably only part of the solution or not a great idea at all. While most of us are not consciously looking for a shortcut, millions of us are looking for a way to earn money without having to change anything about our current life pattern. That standard leaves very little in the way of *real* options.

For example, *some* multi-level marketing companies and "work from home offers" may exploit this longing for a shortcut by promising moms that they can make lots of money and feel a sense of purpose while working only during the kids' nap times and in the few hours of free time a mom has during the day, with just a "small initial investment." While I am a fan of many of the superior products, I see many of these companies profiting from the upfront fees and the first flush of sales made by the moms who take it on with zeal. Months later, the women who might have no sales experience whatsoever are left with a sense of failure (and perhaps with partners who will not let them forget the $1200 of inventory left sitting in the garage) when really it was the wrong choice, for the wrong reasons, all packaged up to look like an appealing shortcut — an easy answer. This can be crushing on an already bruised confidence for moms, and it irritates me to no end that it still happens every day.

Every one of us can probably call to mind that friend who went bonkers over a start-up, a work from home internet offer or plan to resell stuff on Craigslist or just got hired doing "receivables" for some overseas company and was totally convinced that she would earn six figures working a few hours a day. It's agony to watch a friend get excited and feel hopeful and then feel badly about herself later. Maybe you are that woman. I know I have tried my share of shortcuts.

Earning an income is going to be fairly limited if you insist that you can only do so while your kids are napping or at school. Catch yourself when you find that great thing that promises to be the cure-all to your complicated life issues. Ask yourself if you really want to devote your "spare" time to selling whatever the product is without the related sales experience or time. If you decide to do it maybe you get someone to drive carpool a few days a week and devote the time necessary for success. Make sure, if there is a great opportunity, it is great for you first and that your time could not be invested in something even more appealing to you instead. If it looks too good to be true... You know the rest.

Myth: Any decision you make is completely justified if you are at your wit's end and can't take it anymore.

New Rule: Don't make big decisions when you are on the edge.

One of my clients turned up at her son's daycare to find that his caregivers had neglected to put sunscreen on him. He was badly sunburned. Because of his age, she took him to the pediatrician to have him checked out. The doc read her the riot act about how bad daycare centers are and how much the sun exposure had damaged her son's skin, and stopped just short of calling her a neglectful mother. She was plagued with guilt every time she looked at that sweet, red face. Later that night, her husband came home and matter-of-factly announced that he was going to be traveling a lot now as part of his job. In her upset state, she felt like he did not even care that he would be away from their family and believed she would be left to work full-time and tend to their child by herself. Exhausted and hopeless, she woke up the next morning, picked up the phone and quit her $65,000-per-year job without notice.

In the world of coaching, we call this a *reactive decision*. This is not to say that things didn't need to change; it is just that her reaction was not the only solution for the situation. She was in a bad place on a bad day and that can cloud anyone's judgment. It might have been wise to take a time-out from work, to take a few days off to be with her baby and regroup with her husband. There might have been options they could have explored. But hindsight is twenty-twenty as they say. In reality, her husband felt completely left out of the decision to quit her job, which she did without his input (perhaps subconsciously to get back at him for being so casual about *his* career change). And, as a couple, it took some time for them to get back on track while he hunkered down in his travel and she secretly blamed him for not supporting her more. Six months later, she got a new job, found excellent childcare near home, with a much lower ratio of kids to adults and changed her pediatrician as well.

When you feel you are on the edge, remember to control the impulse to change lanes as a reaction to something. You will save time and heartache in the long run by making better and longer lasting decisions. The next time you are fit to be tied, get some sleep (and maybe some sex—it could help), and try to think through all of your options before you change lanes abruptly and drive off the cliff.

Myth: If you are unhappy with your situation you, should change it.
New Rule: Don't measure your current lane by how happy you feel.

As funny as this may sound, you can't really judge the viability of a lane by how happy you or unhappy you are. Happiness may be an important piece of information, but it is only *one* piece of the puzzle because happiness can change dramatically based on the circumstances. One mom told me that she was feeling unhappy and jealous that her childcare provider got to spend the daytime with her kids. One day the caregiver called her at work to report that the family dog had apparently eaten a squirrel and then lost control of his bowels all over the house. The saintly caregiver had put all the kids in the master bedroom with a movie and spent ninety minutes mopping and disinfecting the woman's home. Suddenly the mom realized that while she genuinely wanted to find ways to spend more time with her kids, she certainly did not want to give up her awesome caregiver. Not only did this caregiver take great care of her kids while the woman worked, she took care of her home and made her feel that her house and home were being kept while she was at work. This woman was part of her team.

Another example is a woman who said she felt bored and unchallenged at her job until she found out her husband was having an affair. In the fog of pain and shock that followed, she found a new appreciation for her job, where she was valued for her work and her contribution. She was bored at work, but she was also really good at what she did, and somehow this life change gave her a new appreciation for that work. Work was the one constant in her life at that time, and it helped her get back on track sooner than if she had changed jobs or got involved in a start-up.

Happiness is a big container for a lot of different emotions. How happy you feel can change dramatically based on circumstances. For the time being, let your happiness or unhappiness be a clue to do more digging internally and explore more.

You don't have to endure your unhappiness or ignore it. You may feel unhappy in your marriage, your job or your status as a stay-home mom. Just know that your happiness/unhappiness is part of the total equation of what makes up the right lane for you, your family and your personal wiring. Let your unhappiness be like having a fever on your thermometer. The fever is an indicator, something to cause you to wonder why it is there and what is really going on.

Myth: Your career decisions or professional interests should not upset the flow of things at home.
New Rule: Expect the discomfort of others and communicate it.

If you decide to change lanes at some point in the future, you should anticipate some unrest at home. Even though women are supposed to be the "super-communicators," we frequently make big changes and expect everyone at home to jump on board without discussion or push-back. We make our move this way partially because we don't want the discomfort of our loved ones to make us change our minds. Not only that, but we also feel that our families owe us unquestioned cooperation because we have done so much for them already (can I get an amen?).

I once coached a mother of three who was desperate to go back to work. The economic downturn had hit her family hard and her husband was now working part-time, and their benefits were running out. She had several options she was really excited to explore, but every time she even tried to go on an interview something unforeseen and dramatic would happen at home. Upon further review of the dynamics in her home, it became clear her husband was subtly undermining her efforts to go back to work. Once she realized this, she began to understand that her husband felt emasculated by her decision to go back to work because she had not even discussed it with him. She just figured it was time and that she would get out there and "handle it." Once she realized what was going on, she made time for them to discuss expectations and come to some agreements regarding the upcoming changes before scheduling any more interviews. Things went much smoother after that.

Changing lanes might be the best thing for you and your family, but you will all be better off in the long run if you can anticipate some of the discomfort they may experience and prepare them for the changes. You may not be willing or able to overcome their objections, but at least you will know what they are and will be less likely to change your lane again because everyone is freaking out over fact that mom went back to work, stopped working, went part-time or is taking photos of elephants in Africa and not here next month.

Myth: You made your choice now you have to stick with it.
New Rule: Stay open to the possibilities.

I met a new mom who gave up her work as a scientist when she had her first baby because her husband was a doctor and would never pitch in at home. It's true that he had to work long and erratic hours and that he warned her about it all before they got pregnant. For a long time, she would just repeat the same refrain about her husband never helping and her being stuck at home all day with the kids. If there were any options for her to explore, she would never think of them because she was completely resigned to her situation. She felt stuck, and so she was stuck. Tension between the couple escalated, and they separated for a time. The dynamic between the couple changed during the difficult separation when the husband was forced to handle many of the parenting duties himself during his visits and she was not there to jump in.

Believing that you are trapped in your current work/life situation may feel true but it is not very helpful to think that way. If you find yourself in a situation you wish you could change, then at least allow yourself to think about how things would be in your *ideal* world. I encourage you to let yourself want what you want. Pretend that you are not stuck for awhile. Disable your default settings while you explore options and imagine a life of your choosing. As you explore these thoughts, try and keep it to yourself for a while. Just ponder and wonder. Many ideas and strokes of genius are born of just being open to the possibilities.

A remarkable and true example about the power of staying open to the possibilities is Julie Clark, the inventor of Baby Einstein. Julie was a first grade teacher who decided to stay home after her first child was born. Deep down Julie missed teaching other children about music, poetry and art. As a creative outlet, she shot a video featuring some of the musical concepts she used in her teaching career for her baby. Then, over the next eighteen months she edited the video, working on it only when it was convenient. Later she showed it to others and suddenly the requests started coming in from moms who wanted her video for *their* babies. That video grew to become the famed Baby Einstein Company. This mom left a teaching job that paid $22,000 a year, founded a company, and five years later, the Baby Einstein brand was valued at $22 million. So that's pretty good on the possibilities side.

Maybe you don't want to be a CEO of a multi-million dollar brand but you have a cupcake design idea or want to start a non-profit for people who are in transition. Maybe you just wish you did not have to clean your own home or that you could take a family vacation. Allow yourself to admit what you *want* to be different in your home/career and be willing to quietly explore that.

Are you ready to apply the new rules of the road?

So, which one of the new rules seemed the most surprising to you? Which will be the hardest for you to consider or apply? Which the most liberating? Did any of the examples create an ah-ha or an oh-no inside of your head? Did you dog-ear or mark a page to show your mother-in-law or judgmental co-worker?

You might be amazed now when you notice how often you hear the same old mythology being pedaled as advice to unsuspecting moms — especially new moms. When you hear this, you can choose to enlighten the giver of the crap advice or just relish in the knowledge that you are superior and brilliant for knowing better. All kidding aside, now that you are armed with this information and have done your exercises, it is time to look at The Lanes. Each of the next seven chapters briefly outlines a Career Lane or option. The chapters are short in the hope that can find time to read all of lanes even if you are already committed to your current lane.

NOTES:

NOTES:

PART II

THE LANES

THE LANES

In the next chapters, I will briefly outline each lane and the pros and cons of each. I tell you the truth that nobody else will tell you about that lane. For the most part, any work or career related option can be categorized into one of the lanes. For example, for the moms who declare themselves "stay home" but still want to earn some money can glean information from the stay home chapter (Chapter Three) and the work from home chapter (Chapter Five). The lane chapters are purposely short so that you can read through each lane and organize your thinking around the subject of career and time with your kids. At the end of the pros and cons are three tips for making that particular lane work as well as a look at the best and the worst reasons to pick that lane. The best and worst reasons section is important because when we make career choices from a place of fear or lack or greed, we don't usually get the result we wanted anyway. And that kind of defeats the purpose of picking *that* lane. Once you are clear about what you really want for your family and why that is important to you, then you are less likely to make important decisions from a place of lack or resignation.

" Dear Brenda,

I was not intending to read all of the lanes because well...who has time for that? But I am so glad I did because I learned even more about what I want and what I definitely don't want. The Thinking it Through section at the end of each lane was very helpful and the Three Tips for making that lane work are very useful as well. You might want to encourage your readers to read about all of the lanes."

Jen LaFlam--reader

THE LANES

Chapter Three: The Center Lane
You stay home full-time and your spouse works outside the home

Chapter Four: The Fast Lane
You both work full-time away from home

Chapter Five: The Driveway
You work your job from home

Chapter Six: The Slow Lane
You work part-time, flex-time, job share or reduced hours

Chapter Seven: The Alternative Lane
Your spouse stays home and you work full-time

Chapter Eight: The Turning Lane
You forego income to dedicate time to your education, project, screenplay, novel, etc.

Chapter Nine: The Merge Lane
You both work part-time while sharing childcare and home management equally

CHAPTER THREE

THE CENTER LANE

You stay home full-time and your spouse works outside the home

FYI: Five million moms in the US stay home with their children. In 2010, 23% of married couple family groups with children under the age of fifteen had a mom at home. Source: Pew Research Center.

Many women desire this lane from the depths of their soul. Some women dream of this lane from the very beginning and plan to stay home full-time and care for their children before their children even exist. There is no argument against the consistency that hands-on parenting brings to a family when a parent stays home full-time. Stay home moms get supreme influence over their kids and can powerfully shape the world of their family.

The widely held belief tells mothers that if you *can* afford to stay home, you most certainly should. And commonly accepted wisdom is that the best possible care a child can receive comes from its own mother. These beliefs are packed with the not-so-subtle implication that once you become a mother, any *other* work you may choose to do would pale in comparison to the positive impact you could have on your children by staying home full-time.

This is the lane mothers are "supposed" to want. But common sense tells us that for *any* job, personal wiring and talent for the role impacts the results and outcome dramatically. Not everyone is wired to be an air traffic controller or an operating room nurse or a stay home mom. All of us know that parenting decisions, career choices and relationship issues are complicated and highly personal and that nothing matters more than the quality of the engagement at home or at work. There truly is no right or wrong lane, but if there ever was one track that society overtly "encourages" mothers to take, it is this one. Read this chapter even if you are sure this is not your track, it might help you understand and clarify your own choices.

First we will go through the pros and the cons of this lane. Then I will give you three solid tips for making this lane work and wrap up with an outline called **Thinking it Through** to help you gauge your reasoning and logic when considering this lane.

The Pros of staying home with your kids full-time:

1. **You have maximum influence over what happens to your kids during non-school hours.** In the early years, you have control over what they eat, what they see, hear and do. That influence can be a very impactful parenting tool on many levels. Along with their school teachers, you will be their primary resource for engaging with the world when they are young. As they get older, during the carpools, shuttling to and from sports, homework help and all of the other interactions that you will handle, you will have both subtle and overt influence on their view of the world as well as access to their inner world. That can be a very powerful and rewarding job.

2. **Your cup may runneth over.** You will have good days when you will feel like a mother goddess. Your hard work and attention to detail will result in wonderful moments spent watching the most important people in your world progress and thrive, largely because of your efforts. This feels great, and their accomplishments may help convince you that it is worth all of the hard work you put in.

3. **Scheduling is less complicated.** Taking the work related push-and-pull off the table (for one parent) can certainly make things much simpler on many levels, and scheduling tops the list. Anyone who

has a child knows how busy life is for kids in today's world. Parents and many experts alike believe that kids are overscheduled these days, and there is some credence to that. However, kids do play more sports, participate in more activities, and have greater opportunities for enrichment then they used to, and that can be a good thing. While there is nothing simple about parenting—regardless of your lane choice—it is helpful not to have to accommodate anyone's schedule but your own, and of course your kids'.

4. **You will not have to deal with work-related annoyances.** There is a peace derived from not having to deal with the downside of the business world. Of course, this depends entirely on what you used to do for a living, but for most people, "work" comes with at least a small dosage of something unpleasant. For many, a large, steaming pile of unpleasantness is served up daily. Perhaps it's annoying office politics, a dysfunctional boss, a greedy board, work overwhelm, gender inequity, sexual harassment, eternal meetings or the constant threat of layoffs. It can be tough out there in the business world on some days, and not being part of it can be a good thing.

5. **Roles are clearer.** There is simplicity inherent in this choice. Your partner works and makes money while you stay home with the kids. Don't confuse "simple" with "easy" though. There is no "easy" when it comes to kids. Still, things are less complicated, and that can be good. Moms in a household where both partners work will tell you how frustrating it is to feel like they do everything at home—even though they work too. While there may still be way too much to do, in this lane you will be clear about who does what.

The Cons of staying home with your kids full-time:

1. **Your family is solely dependent upon one income/job,which allows for fewer options.** This means that if things get unsettled at work for your spouse, your family will have less in the way of backup plans and choices. It makes your family beholden to his work

situation. Being beholden can feel like enslavement. If the company moves the home office to Omaha, that likely means you are moving to Omaha with your babies (or much worse, your teenagers). Moms who have even a little income can often ramp that up if it becomes necessary (like it did for millions when the economy went haywire recently). But for those moms who don't have any income, it is hard to start from scratch should they suddenly need to become the breadwinner or contribute more. This is no reason for a stay home mom to get a part-time job "just in case" something happens. That would be making decisions from a place of fear. But it is important to understand that if you say goodbye to your career now, you will have fewer choices if faced with a sudden change.

2. **People say raising kids is the hardest job in the world, but** *they don't mean it.* If you are a stay home mom, many people will wonder openly what you "do" all day. Sorry, but it is true. The pressure on mothers to be perfect, raise perfect children and look perfect all the while is absurd. But what makes this even worse is that everyone, from child experts to talk show hosts to your mother-in-law, will tell you that raising kids is the "hardest and most important job in the world" out of one side of their mouths and then devalue that work out of the other side. Mothers are not stupid. We can see what the world values: money, success, beauty, material gain, industry and accomplishment. Just remember that when you are waiting for societal kudos for the sacrifices you are making, they aren't coming.

3. **Your spouse may think that he works harder than you do.** I have been talking to husbands of stay home moms on my business trips for over fifteen years. The truth is that many of these gents think their wives have it made and are "living the dream" while the husbands are out there killing themselves to make a living. As a result of this widely held belief, your partner might not pitch in on anything that he considers *your* job. He may tell you he needs to golf or play softball every Saturday to relieve stress from *his* job. It should

be noted that I have also talked to many guys who respect their stay home wives' work and sacrifice and who miss their kids painfully while they are traveling or working. So be aware that opinions on who works harder can vary. Some partners may need to be reminded to consider the number of children, the impossible hours of motherhood, the requirements of kids with special needs, teenagers, school struggles, etc.

4. **If you are cutting costs in order to stay home with your kids, it will limit their activities as well.** Not that kids need everything—because they don't. But keep in mind that if you are giving up a yearly income to stay home, then you may not be able to involve your kids in things they might otherwise get to do. For example, some kids need social interaction at a young age and can benefit from preschool or a couple years of Montessori or art class. Many stay home moms plan to fill in the gaps with their own time and attention; however, areas like language acquisition, sports-specific training, special needs tutors, music lessons, swimming, etc., all cost extra and might not be your specialty. Later, if you tell your kids that you staying home with them is a great trade-off for space camp or acting lessons, they will tell you to get a job.

5. **Your spouse might not get much time with your kids.** In the 1950s when this whole stay home mother concept was delivered to us in Technicolor, the dads pretty much worked eight-hour days and most did not have much in the way of business travel, corporate retreats, training classes, pressure to get an MBA or the threat of corporate take-over bearing down on them. Today's income earner is practically considered part-time if he or she works "only" a forty-hour week. The reality of applying this more traditional parenting model to today's work structure is that you will get a little too much time with the kiddies and he will not get enough. You may feel like all he does is work, and all you do is take care of the kids. Unless you have a very unique situation, you will probably be right.

6. **The longer you stay home, the harder it will be to go back to work.**
   Many moms pick this lane with the idea that they will stay home
   until their youngest child starts school. The reality is it can add up
   to more years than you may think. Many kids do not go to school all
   day until age four or five. If you have three kids who are each two
   years apart, that is already nine years! Even if you stay home for
   just five years, that is a long time away from a career. And once the
   kids are in school and you decide to get a job, you will realize that
   having kids in school does not allow for as much work time as you
   might think. You will likely only have from 10:00am until 2:00pm to
   actually work. Most jobs aren't scheduled that way. Plus, everyone
   at home will be used to you doing lots of things for them and might
   resist you. None of the above is insurmountable; however, the combination of factors can make moms feel like the odds are stacked
   against them.

Three Tips For Making This Lane Work:

1. **Focus on making your kids and family as independent as possible**. Of course, doing everything for our kids is not just a problem
   for stay home moms. We all do it. But it's a bigger temptation for
   stay home moms because after all — you are home. Be sure to do
   your work in Chapter Ten (Division of Labor) and check that list.
   See where some investment is necessary to make your kids more
   independent and self-sufficient. It might not be too late.

2. **Insist on time for yourself each day.** This is in addition to your exercise workout. This means getting some childcare so that you can
   explore your creativity, your intellect or simply the world beyond
   children. If you really want to be valued for what you do, *you* have
   to value what you do and insist on some regular breaks regardless
   of inconvenience. Usually, the only person you will have to convince is yourself. This short-term guilt will pay off in the long run

when you feel more empowered, less resentful and truly have a life of your own in addition to being a mom.

3. **Push yourself to be "out there."** Moms who get out of the habit of being "out in the world" have a harder time readjusting in the event that they unexpectedly need or want to go back to work. Find a way to be "in the world" and perhaps even a little out of your comfort zone. Resist the temptation to isolate or surround yourself only with other stay home moms or to let your mothering role become 100% of your world. Esteem often gets eroded over time, but conversely, it can be enhanced or preserved by putting ourselves "out there" little by little and feeling the satisfaction of having done something that builds confidence. Being out in the world can mean taking a class in a subject of interest, networking, volunteering in an area that is not connected to your kids or family, attending workshops or learning a trade.

Thinking It Through

YOU MIGHT WANT TO CONSIDER THIS LANE IF...	YOU MIGHT WANT TO PASS ON THIS LANE IF...	CAUTION SIGNS-SLOW DOWN, CONSIDER OTHER OPTIONS BEFORE PROCEEDING...
You truly, truly want to do this role and it is financially feasible.	It would wreak havoc on your finances but you don't care because you want to do it so badly.	Sometimes we get blinded by desire. It's okay to want to stay home and it's also okay to not wreck your life to do it. If you really cannot afford it, you might explore options for being "mostly" home.

You have children with someone who really "gets you." Who understands the sacrifice you are making and the value that you add by not keeping a traditional job during this life phase.	Staying home full-time is a family tradition and you feel pushed or pressured or "guilted" into this role by your spouse, family, your religious community or society.	Keep in mind that you will be giving up a lot of freedom and options by staying home. How you *really* feel about it will have a huge impact on how well it goes for you and your kids, so be careful not to do it out of pressure from others.
This choice to stay home aligns with your lifestyle choice of using less resources or sustainability.	You secretly hate your job and you have convinced yourself that having time to be home will save a fortune because you will make your own soap and candles and clean the house and cut the lawn etc.	Be careful if you are justifying the loss of income with the number of things you will do with your own physical labor at home as you will be with your kids and the days fly by. You might save on water usage, however, since you won't have time to shower as often as you might like.
You have a unique work situation where, at least from a job standpoint, you can actually leave for an extended period of time and then have the flexibility to pick up where you left off.	You are making this decision because if you worked, you would make the same amount or less money than it would cost for daycare.	Mom's income will grow over time and childcare costs will actually go down. A willingness to look at your real reasons for wanting to stay home is key if you are going to "do the math" on staying home. See **Chapter Two**: *Shifting Gears*
You realize that you will still need to rely on others since you cannot work 24/7 as a mother.	You are making this decision because you are terrified to leave your child in the care of someone else and you are plagued by images of all of the things that could happen.	Making a decision from a place of fear will almost never bring you the peace you seek (I hate that!). See **Chapter One**: *Checking Under The Hood*
You are investing in your kids, and while it is a lot to give from your standpoint, it is not too much to give.	You don't want to miss a thing and don't want your kid's "firsts" to be seen by some babysitter or teacher.	Lots of working parents get plenty of time with their kids and see lots of "firsts" as well. Don't make the decision out of "parental greed."

You are wired for this role and your strengths lie in coping with the most stressful aspects of staying home, namely: repetition, monotony, frustration, thanklessness, repetition, monotony, frustration, thanklessness repetition, monotony, frustration, thanklessness.	In order to stay home, you are going to have to "shelve" many aspects of yourself like being a type A personality, having a competitive nature, a powerful ambition for success and/or being driven to get results in everything you do.	We all have powerful drives in one direction or another. Some drives are better suited to stay home motherhood and others are best channeled elsewhere.

Jot down a few lines on your impressions of this lane. Did you have any realizations? Could you be a stay home mom? Any tweaks you want to make in your current lane?

Notes, thoughts and questions about this lane:

There is no influence so powerful as that of the mother.

-Sarah Josepha Hale

NOTES:

CHAPTER FOUR

THE FAST LANE

You both work full-time away from home.

FYI: According to data collected by the U.S. Bureau of Labor Statistics, 59% of women now work or are actively seeking employment. An even higher percentage of women with children ages 17 or younger, (66%) work either full or part-time. **Among those working mothers, most (74%) work full-time** *while 26% work part-time.*

Working full-time *and* being a mother can be powerful and heady stuff. It's funny when you think about the fact that women had to earn the right to work just like we had to earn the right to legally own property, get a higher education, vote and marry someone of our choosing. Sadly, in many pla-ces around the globe, women are still being denied these rights, and in other places, women are forced to do life-threatening work day and night in an attempt to earn pennies to feed and protect their families. But here in North America, much of South America and most of Europe, women are running companies, departments, territories, meetings and projects while also parenting, being domestic and occasionally romantic. More than half of the moms reading this book can "bring home the bacon and fry it up in a pan.

But there is still controversy about working moms and the term "full-time working mom" is a headline in and of itself. Men get no such attention for being full-time working fathers—heck, in the whole what's-best-for-children parenting media controversy, men hardly exist.

And of course, it is especially heart-wrenching that most of the judgment against working moms now comes from other moms. Yet millions of moms go to work every day and still, somehow, manage to keep their families from going to hell in a hand basket.

Surprisingly the major stress for full-time working moms will *not* come from feeling judged by the hypocrites in the media who are peddling advice they don't practice themselves. No, it comes instead from a lethal combination of self-inflicted guilt, impossible standards, poor division of labor at home and prideful refusal to get the help they need. But these are all fixable things. Read on and see if full-time work is for you now or some time in future.

First we will go through the pros and the cons of this lane. Then I will give you three solid tips for making this lane work and wrap up with an outline called **Thinking it Through** to help you gauge your reasoning and logic when considering this lane.

The Pros of working full-time away from home:

1. **It feels powerful to work full-time *and* be a mother**. Work can be very empowering, and continuing to work full-time, earn an income *and* raise a family is a bit of an ego boost. For many moms, work is so much more than the income. Work can be a creative expression, a way of serving the greater good, a chance to put your skills to good use, or simply a right, necessity or choice. The self-esteem boost that can be generated from outer-world kudos for a working woman in today's society should not be underestimated.

2. **More money now *and* later.** In most cases, the more working people there are in a household, the more money there is. And if you work consistently throughout the child rearing years, your income tends to increase over time, while childcare costs tend to go down as your children grow up.

3. **You will have more leverage at home.** Work is an equalizer in a love relationship (especially if your mate is a man), so full-time work is the ultimate equalizer. Being able to say, "Hey, I have a full-time job too!" can be very helpful in the division of duties department at home. I am not saying it will help your case for domestic equality, but at least you get to say it.

4. **You will be modeling independence to your children.** Working was not always an option for women. We have come a long way since a high court in the State of Illinois upheld a law stating, "The paramount destiny and mission of women is to fulfill the noble and benign offices of wife and mother."1873: *Bradwell v. Illinois.* After this history, it is still kind of cool to show kids that mom can work as well as parent.

5. **You and your partner will have more in common.** The typical ups and downs of work can be a point of connection and foster a sense of teamwork in your relationship. When things are tough as well as when they are flowing smoothly at your job, it's nice to share that with a partner who can relate and even offer advice.

The Cons of working full-time away from home:

1. **You will still do more than your fair share of the housework.** Yep. That's right. According to the Bureau of Labor Statistics, in 2009 married mothers who were employed full-time were more likely to do household activities—such as housework, cooking, or lawn care—on an average day than were fathers who were employed full-time (89 versus 64 percent). Do you think the inequity is because he makes more money? Think again. Even women who out-earn their husbands still do more than half of the housework.

2. **You will have to depend on others to help care for your children.** This plan comes with more burning hoops and juggling than Cirque du Soleil! This is what really wipes out working moms physically and mentally. Problems start when something goes wrong with one

of the multiple channels of help you have arranged. Child minding is not an area where you want to take chances on poor quality, so it can get expensive. But more expensive does not *always* mean better quality. Full-time working moms have to deal with many changes in this arena as their kids grow, and it can be taxing.

3. **You will miss *some* important moments.** While staying home can sometimes be *too much* of a good thing, working full-time outside the home can be *not enough* of a good thing. Depending on the nature of your work, you simply may not be present for *every* first step, *every* game and *every* performance for *every* one of your children.

4. **People might think you are a heartless bitch.** For some reason, there are lots of unimaginative people who assume that moms who work full-time only care about expensive cars and power jobs. It's a double standard, certainly, but you might get to see this rampant bias play out if you choose this lane.

5. **Sometimes you will feel like you are being pulled in opposite directions.** This is because you are. Work and motherhood should not be opposing, but often they are just that. Even enjoyable and rewarding work can be all consuming at times, and in today's world, forty hours seems like part-time (to employers). Add to this a working mom's tendency to blame everything that goes wrong on the fact that she works (even when it is not true), and you have a recipe for major stress. It can be very difficult even if you like your job. And if you hate your job, this can be hell for everyone in your household, especially you.

6. **You and your spouse might become two ships passing in the night.** Some of the ways that you might balance work and family (like tag-teaming so that one of you is always home with the kids) will be tough on your relationship. Especially when the kids are little it may feel like there is no "adult time" for you and your spouse.

Three Tips For Making This Lane Work:

1. **Expect pitfalls and make back-up plans.** Confirmation that this lane is working will *not* be the absence of things going wrong. Things can and will go wrong with the many moving parts in this equation, but that is life. Get in the habit of making contingency plans and get your spouse and kids in the habit of doing this as well. Life has enough surprises as it is, but childcare falling through, one of the kids getting sick on the day of your big presentation, forgotten lunches and car trouble should be part of your back-up plan because it's not a matter of if it will happen — it's when. While you cannot spend your life making back-up plans, you can keep a good friend on-call in case something comes up on big, non-negotiable work days, hide $10 in your kids' back pack in case they forget lunch and sign up for 24-hour roadside assistance if you have an old car.

2. **Learn to delegate, hire help and/or lower your standards**. Doing everything yourself in a perfect way plus working full-time outside the home is simply not a sustainable plan. Even if you can do it for a while, often the real benefits of work come over time, and at that kind of pace, you might not last. Keep in mind that lowering standards and getting help does not mean you have to give up all control or live in a pigsty. Sometimes it will be better to write a check for the class party at your child's school rather than volunteer to plan it. Sometimes you will need to hire a lawn company or cleaning company, or you'll need to have the birthday party at the easiest place (not your house) this time around.

3. **Pay attention to your marriage and schedule some family time.** Maybe it's an occasional date with your spouse and/or a monthly family night where cell phones are banned and the board games come out. You probably don't need as much dedicated marriage and family time as you might think, but paying attention is crucial to marital survival in this lane. If the thought of a date with your husband or harnessing the kids for an evening sounds like a huge

pain, then you probably need it more than ever. And don't expect immediate cooperation from the involved parties—the benefit of face-time comes over time.

Thinking It Through

YOU MIGHT WANT TO CONSIDER THIS LANE IF...	YOU MIGHT WANT TO PASS ON THIS LANE IF...	CAUTION SIGNS-SLOW DOWN, CONSIDER OTHER OPTIONS BEFORE PROCEEDING...
You are in a profession that does not lend itself to part-time or flex-time right now (or ever) and this makes sense to you at this point and time.	You are choosing this lane primarily because you need the money, even though you hate your job or hate the fact that you are NOT home with your kids.	It's none of anyone's business why you work full-time and there is no reason you should have to justify it. But feeling trapped and hating your job could wear on you over time in a way that makes it not worth it in the first place. Explore other options first.
In choosing this lane, you are acknowledging that you are willing to do what it takes to get excellent childcare and help. You and your spouse fully understand that in order to sustain your union and your sanity, you are going to need assistance from the outside world.	You are essentially anti-childcare but you are going to try to "work-it-out" between the two of you, enlist the help of neighbors and/or do the tag-team thing indefinitely	In reality this plan will not work for long. Your neighbors will stop taking your calls, and your family may not always be ideal or available caregivers. And really, is this flimsy set-up "better" than childcare? Also, you will put your work and your marriage at risk if you try to do the tag-team for very long simply because you will never see your spouse. Full-time, working parents need regular, high quality help.

You have long-term plans for the future that include you continuing to work.	You are working full-time because, otherwise, your husband will stick you with all of the house and kid stuff forever, or because you are afraid he will lose respect for you if you don't work full-time like he does.	Many couples form their opinions about kids and work and division of labor BEFORE they have kids and then don't revisit the assumptions after the reality of kids sets in. It's important to take time to discuss your current reality and make a new plan— together.
You have an employment situation that is truly "family friendly"[1], flexible or otherwise motivating you to continue for now. Or your employer really "gets you" and your work provides some special, *useful* perks to your family (such as air-travel credits or free access to amusement parks or healthcare contributions).	You are afraid your job won't be there if you quit or reduce your hours.	I have talked to hundreds of women who had initially planned to quit work after their kids came, but their super smart employers instead found a way to keep them. This is why each mom has to think about her individual set-up. But staying at work because you are afraid it will go away won't actually get you what you want in the end. See Chapter Two: *Shifting Gears*

---

[1] Many companies tout themselves as family friendly but really are not. For example companies may have company paid childcare for employees' children but the culture dictates that everyone work fourteen-hour days. That is family tolerant, not family friendly. Family friendly by our definition is a company or employer that actually allows people to have time, money or perks that extend to the children and spouse of the employee and allow the time to use such benefits or flexibility.

What are your beliefs and thoughts about working full-time outside of the home? What would the ideal situation be for you to choose this lane? Are you in this lane but feel trapped?

Notes, thoughts and questions about this lane:

I think it's a false trade-off to say quality time vs. quantity – you have to have both. So if you have long work hours like I did, how do you get rid of things in your life you don't need in order to put that extra time into your children? I always supported the women I worked with having time off to go to parent-teacher conferences and doctors' appointments or bringing their infant into the office.
-US Secretary of State, Hillary Rodham Clinton

NOTES:

NOTES:

CHAPTER FIVE

THE DRIVEWAY

You work your job from home

According to the Telework Research Network, twenty to thirty million people currently work from home at least one day a week in the US. Fifteen to twenty million are road warriors/mobile workers; ten to fifteen million are home businesses; fifteen to twenty million work at home part-time (with about half doing so one to two days a week); and about three million are based at home full-time.

One of the greatest things about working from home is that you get to keep some of your domestic tasks moving along while still getting lots of work done for your job. Lucky telecommuters get to throw in a load of laundry instead of having an impromptu "chat" with that co-worker who never, ever stops talking. You get to pop on the TV and catch the news or a Hollywood gossip show while quickly finishing last night's dishes instead of attending several of the tortuous meetings that the auditor from corporate has scheduled for your co-workers this week. And depending on your job, you may be able to stop working in the afternoon so that you can pick up your kids from school, attend a soccer practice and then finish work later. Working from home can be ideal.

Depending on your industry, telecommuting may become a reality for you whether you choose it or not. Technology as well as other employees' demands for flexibility have a huge impact on employers' decisions to allow telecommuting and provide remote access to the company network. But nothing has a larger impact than the fact that companies are saving millions of dollars by closing or streamlining offices and sending their employees home to work. Oftentimes people who had no intention of working from home are faced with the sudden need to do so.

Telecommuters often complain that they feel like they are working 24/7. And they're not imagining it. The work-from-home employment option has contributed significantly to the cultural phenomenon of working around the clock because the lines between work and domesticity are blurred. Work, family and chores are all endless. Ironically it's the super disciplined workers and devoted parents that will suffer the most. Pre-dawn email and conference calls are followed by the morning routine with the kids and then back to the desk for more work. Then it's afternoon and time to pick up kids, throw in an errand or two, manage sports and after school events with the laptop fired up and calls being handled in hallways and at the back door of the gym. Then there is dinner and a throbbing inbox, the workout you promised yourself and oh yeah — sex with your spouse.

First we will go through the pros and the cons of this lane. Then I will give you three solid tips for making this lane work and wrap up with an outline called **Thinking it Through** to help you gauge your reasoning and logic when considering this lane.

The Pros of working from home

1. **The flexibility is great.** Work from home moms can do many of the things that stay home moms can do while still earning an income. In most cases you can work a bit before the kids wake up (or after they go to bed if you are a night person) and then be involved in morning activities before getting back to work. You can often arrange your other breaks to coincide with a car pool, game or event. And yes, my clever friend, this "flexibility" will appear in the cons section of this chapter as well.

2. **You get to skip some of the office politics and boring meetings.** Life can be quite blissful when you don't have to spend time on office politics, lunches and meetings because you are not physically

available to people. You will be amazed at how much more "pure" work gets done without the entire office engaging you. And less time spent on that stuff usually translates to more time with your kids even if you work from home full-time.

3. **In the right role, income can be surprisingly high in this segment of the job market.** Remarkably, working from home does not necessitate lowering your income. Depending on what you do for a living, working from home can pay as well or better than working in an office. Outside sales representatives have been doing this for decades. If you can find ways to maximize productivity and get into a groove, you may earn more than you did at the office.

4. **It can feel like the best of both worlds**. There is a reason that people are jealous of those with this work/family combination. Staying involved in the details of your kids' lives while earning an income and contributing to something outside of your family can be a rewarding experience.

5. **Less attention to wardrobe, commuting, etc.** There is a certain ecology that comes with not having to put gas in your car as often, not having to dry clean your clothes, and having a few days per week that are shower optional. With this option, you will wear out your pajamas and workout wear faster, even though you might not be getting more exercise (or sleep).

The Cons of working from home

1. **Your spouse may consider you a stay home mom who magically produces income, seemingly without having to work**. If you go this route, you will have to fight for your right to actually work. Don't laugh—it's true. There is no shortage of "stuff" to do in your home and your spouse is less likely to pitch in and do his part if you are in the house. Also, your spouse, who may have to commute daily or jump on and off airplanes might think you have it easier

even if you work as much or more than he does and even if you earn more.

2. **You will feel like you work four to five shifts a day.** This is actually both an upside and a downside of this program. On one hand it is great that you can usually change something at the drop of a hat, but it's also a detriment because work not attended to during the day ends up being done in the night or wee hours of the morning, and that can get old. Even on great days it is a bit dizzying to start and stop all the time. If you compare a straightforward twelve-hour day at work vs. six hours of work mixed in with six hours of off-and-on family care, domesticity and driving, you will see how exhausting it is. The straight twelve at work, doing one thing, is actually much less tiring.

3. **If you do not have childcare, you will likely feel like a failure at both jobs.** If you work from home, you may find that your new "co-workers" are a bunch of clingy, screaming kids who are in desperate need of supervision. The point is that you are likely to require some regular childcare in this equation even if it conflicts with your financial hopes and goals. Working from home while minding the kids makes it very difficult to concentrate on either work or your kids very well for very long. So if you are going this route to save on childcare costs, you might want to re-think it.

4. **Little social contact.** It's important that you know yourself to be a person who can live without the regular social contact associated with working outside the home. Most work-from-homers relish work life and spend enough time interacting on the phone or in meetings to need only minimal additional social contact. But some moms really miss being in the mix and feel isolated at home. Social interaction is a big thing to live without if you need it.

5. **Out of sight, out of mind at work.** Being a woman who works from home is one thing, but being a "mom" who works from home can be another thing entirely. If you are one who initiated the work-from-home

idea at your job you may have some extra public relations tasks to do to keep your work, and your reputation, on the positive side of the balance sheet in the minds of your employers. Just as your spouse might think you have it easier, so might your bosses and co-workers.

Three Tips For Making This Lane Work:

1. **Learn to set boundaries.** Your success in this lane depends almost entirely on your ability to actually *work* from home. Working from home probably does not mean that you can do 100% of the domestic and kid stuff and still produce. That is impossible. Figure out what you need as far as quiet time, childcare, phone time, etc. and see to it that you get it. Not easy but necessary.

2. **Give the concept time to work.** It takes time to learn to master this lane. I tell clients to give it a year if they are working from home for the first time. It's an adjustment to be productive, go without social interaction, and keep your kids from taking up 115% of your time. Even the location of your office/equipment and supplies might require an adjustment at first. Be careful not to set a precedence of doing things you cannot sustain over the long haul and try different approaches to see what fits and what does not. Be sure to reach out to others who are already successfully working from home.

3. **Be strategic about your interactions with co-workers or clients.** Be conscious of the perceptions about you at work and manage those perceptions, because you will have significantly fewer opportunities to impress people than you would if you were there in person. Be on time or early for meetings or conference calls and make sure you have coverage for your kids (and back-up coverage) for important meetings. Pay special care to look professional and rested when you do see co-workers and be cognizant of background noise from pets, kids and doorbells when participating in conference calls or webinars from your home office.

Thinking It Through

YOU MIGHT WANT TO CONSIDER THIS LANE IF...	YOU MIGHT WANT TO PASS ON THIS LANE IF...	CAUTION SIGNS-SLOW DOWN, CONSIDER OTHER OPTIONS BEFORE PROCEEDING...
You have the perfect setup at home and your company is open to the idea or already has it in place for other workers.	You are opting to work from home so that you can save money on childcare.	You will still need childcare—perhaps more than ever. If you are in doubt, try this: tomorrow at the office while you are working on a really important task, set your alarm to go off every two minutes, when the alarm goes off, jump up and do something completely unrelated to that task and then go back to that task. Now do that every day for 5 days straight and you have a typical mom at home—trying to work while attending to her family.
You know your job like the back of your hand and can do it from anywhere.	You are secretly using this as a stepping-stone to quitting your job entirely and hoping to somehow morph into no work at all instead of admitting the truth and making a plan to do so.	Be honest if you hate dislike your work and are over it. You deserve a more honest and ethical parting from your employer and so might your employer.
You have the gift of focus and you can step over dirty laundry, ignore the house phone and work—even with dishes in the sink.	You are choosing this because your company offers it and you feel you should take advantage of it for your kids' sake, but you do not really want to work from home or you know you will really miss the social contact.	Working from home successfully requires a tremendous amount of discipline so you really have to be wired for it. Plus employers tend to watch work-from-home employees more closely and will be looking for clues to how much work is getting done while you are home with your family.

Who do you know that works from home and what does their life seem like to you? Which pro or con surprised you the most? Notes, thoughts and questions about this lane:

Like all working mothers, sometimes I feel like a terrible mother and sometimes I feel like a terrible employee. But for the most part, I try to give myself a break, which is something I urge all mothers to do – to live your life with a cloud of guilt about everything you are doing is just not good for anybody.

-Katie Couric

NOTES:

CHAPTER SIX

THE SLOW LANE

You work part-time, flex-time, job share or reduced hours

From 1997 to 2007 the Pew Research Study found that, among the participants, part-time work is the preferred option of about half of mothers who work full-time and a third of mothers who don't work outside the home.

This lane, working any variation of part-time, is often touted as the best of both worlds. Mom gets to keep her job, earn income and not miss a beat at home. And certainly anyone who has done it will tell you that it has its benefits especially if you can manage to truly work part-time. It can feel quite ideal because you earn an income, possibly keeping your options open should you need to go to a full-time schedule *and* are involved in your kids daily lives much more than you would be if you worked full-time. Child minding is less monotonous because you get to pause for work at the allotted time or day, and then work halts in the service of picking up the kids, running errands, attending a mom group or exercising.

It may surprise you to know that of all the moms I interviewed for this book, the moms working part-time or flex-time are the most frustrated and are often unhappy. It is possible that this is due to unrealistic expectations on the part of everyone involved: the mom, the employer and the spouse. Of all the lanes, this is the one that moms jump into without paying *enough* attention to the math on all sides of the equation. Not just the math of losing income by going from full-time to part-time, but more importantly, the reality that in most cases moms who "cut down" to part-time end up doing a full-time job in half the time for half the money. Not to mention the fact that they do most of the heavy lifting at home. Whoops.

Job share, part-time and flex-time are actually fantastic options but only to the extent that the mom understands what skills she can leverage at work and what she can realistically accomplish at home. The key word is leverage. Men seemed to be wired for leveraging situations to meet their needs and desires. But women have a harder time thinking that way. Without really considering all the angles, we get excited about the possibilities of part-time then we march into our boss's office and offer to take half of our pay for half the hours (I am getting a rash even as I type this). The "happier" moms were strategic about negotiation with their employers before committing to part-time.

If you are thinking of going part-time now or after your baby is born, start by making a list of the key things you do at work and then a list of things the company could have someone else do. Then talk about money and hours in terms of the value you bring to the equation. Offer to do the aspects of your job that are more valuable and impactful and ask for more income (a larger portion than half of your full-time income) than you would get if you were doing the other tasks. The ideal math for this "ideal set-up" is that you get more than half of your pay for part-time because you are condensing full-time work into fewer hours and doing way more than half of the job. And you are giving your company what they need — you.

Note: If you work your part-time job from home and you skipped right to this chapter go back and read Chapter 5 as well.

First we will go through the pros and the cons of this lane. Then I will give you three solid tips for making this lane work and wrap up with an outline called **Thinking it Through** to help you gauge your reasoning when considering this lane.

The Pros of working part-time, flex-time or job share

1. **This can be the best of both worlds**. You are generating income, possibly getting healthcare benefits for your family, and you still have the flexibility to do much of the parenting. Your kids' schedule and needs will change often, and this is the lane that will let you tweak as you go. Awesome.

2. **Often you can turn this into full-time income if you need to**. During the economic downturn of 2008, millions of moms who worked part-time were able to go full-time when their husbands lost their income, a lane switch that literally saved some family homes. The economists coined the term "man-cession" referring to loss of jobs among men, which occurred at a higher rate than it did among their female counterparts.

3. **You are demonstrating two very good things to your children**. Your kids will see you work and manage your family. Of course they won't appreciate it or verbalize it, but the lessons will not be lost.

4. **The variety can be wonderful**. Moms report feeling very empowered by this option because they get to vary their activities and can show up to school and sports events while also taking time in the same day to be productive in their work role. It can be liberating to have neither your role as a parent nor your role at work totally dominate or define your existence.

5. **You can be more focused at work**. If you only go into the office on Monday, Wednesday and Friday, for example, there is a stronger sense of urgency about your work, which can keep you more focused. Also, you can more easily justify saying no to team lunches and other work functions (if you want to) as you have so much to do in so little time.

The Cons of working part-time, flex-time or job share

1. **You might condense a full-time job into less pay and have fewer hours to accomplish it.** Many women negotiate "part-time" with their employer and give up half or more of their pay only to find that the remainder of the job has not been reassigned. Thus, you could be doing your whole job for half the pay in half the time allowed. Not fun!

2. **Your husband may not respect your work as much as if you worked full-time.** In his mind, his full-time job will take precedence, and your part-time work is less important. This will mean more housework, carpooling, etc. will fall on you, even though you may work and/or earn plenty and your flexible schedule may create all kinds of benefits for your family.

3. **The intensity of part-time work and part-time domesticity can be very tiring.** Frankly, it is easier to either just work twelve hours straight or be domestic for twelve hours. But interchanging between the two, round the clock, can be exhausting. And sometimes it's hard to leave the office at your appointed time if you are working part-time when you know you will not be back for several days. While this choice is a popular one for parents, it is actually harder than it may seem if you always feel tired or frustrated.

4. **When your kids get sick, your job is in jeopardy.** Many people pick this track so that they can stay home when their kids get sick or be there when their kids need them. But if you really think about it, that makes no sense. If you work three days a week and your kid is sick on one of those days, you are missing one-third of your work week, or two-thirds if you are out for two days. Part- time work does not mean you can drop your work and respond to every family need, so you will still need back-up childcare or some way of making up lost time to your employer if you want to keep your job.

5. **Childcare is necessary but harder to get in the time frame you need it.** Most moms who work part-time often end up paying for

full-time childcare because the system is set up for full-time workers. This can make paying for childcare even harder to justify.

Three Tips For Making This Lane Work

1. **Do the math.** If you are considering approaching your employer about moving from full-time to part-time, make a list of the key things you do at work and what value (monetary and otherwise) your work brings to the company. Next make a list of the parts of your job you think it would be wisest to give up or that you could farm out to someone else in the company. Think of things from their perspective, keeping in mind the results the company will most be focused on achieving. And don't just give up half of your pay for half of the hours if it might not even be necessary. At home map out income, what hours you will work, who will do what at home, cost of childcare, etc., and make sure it is actually doable. And it's never too late to do this math. If you have been doing everything at home, plus working a part-time job, you can still re-negotiate with everyone.

2. **Get reliable childcare.** Sure it costs money and might take up some of your now reduced income. But if you want your part-time work schedule to last, you are going to need some help. If anyone has used the words *haggard, scattered, disheveled, or exhausted* to describe you recently, you need childcare. You can be creative about this, but it is necessary and it needs to be reliable. One mom who worked part-time as a hair stylist had one of her three kids in school, one in a licensed daycare and her newborn with a share-nanny on the days she worked. The mom felt that each child needed something different for his or her developmental stage. In months when work was slow, she paid out more than she earned but there were also several times over the years that her husband got laid-off and she increased her hours. Her childcare set-up allowed her husband to devote himself full-time to his job search while she earned more income.

3. **Get some YOU time ASAP.** Of all the lanes, this one is the one that will provide you the least YOU time because everyone in your life thinks you have it made—including your employer. Make yourself a priority and find some alone time, grooming time and time to nurture your friendships and your relationship with your spouse. But you first. Everyone will benefit.

Thinking It Through

YOU MIGHT WANT TO CONSIDER THIS LANE IF…	YOU MIGHT WANT TO PASS ON THIS LANE IF…	CAUTION SIGNS-SLOW DOWN, CONSIDER OTHER OPTIONS BEFORE PROCEEDING…
Your brilliant employer wants to keep you and is open to a myriad of schedule possibilities.	Your spouse doesn't help so you are cutting back to part-time to spite him.	Show your partner the math of you keeping your job full-time over the next few years. Perhaps instead of giving up half of your income, maybe it's cheaper to hire some help with the house and/or use a food delivery service, pet care person etc.
You can make great money without full-time effort or you simply want to do your job less.	You hate your job, so less of it sounds better than all of it.	It depends on why you hate your job. If it's the people then less time at work might help but if it is the work then you are only delaying the inevitable. Less of a bad thing is still a bad thing.
You have a great idea for a proposal to demonstrate how your employer can win, you can win and your family can win.	Your spouse won't "let" you quit work so you are cutting back as much as you can.	You and your spouse might benefit from some time discussing options. Find a time when you are rested and having a good day and come up with at least five new options before you agree to part-time work.

What surprises you about the pros and cons of this lane? If you are con-sidering this lane what is your primary reason? Do you know others who are in this lane? Notes, thoughts and questions about this lane:

....

....

....

....

....

....

....

If I'm not doing any job at 120 percent, I think I'm failing. So if you're trying to do that at home and at work, you find it very difficult and stressful and frustrating.

-Michelle Obama

NOTES:

CHAPTER SEVEN

THE ALTERNATIVE LANE

Your spouse stays home and you work full-time.

The number of stay-at-home dads has grown over 60 percent since 2004. A recent Pew Research Center study called "Women, Men and the New Economics of Marriage" revealed that women are making much more money, over the recent past, than at any other time in our history. The country's stay-at-home dads number approximately 165,000.

Things have come a long way with dads if you think about it. As recently as the 1970s, fathers were relegated to the hospital waiting room while their wives delivered babies in a sterile haze of ether and forceps (yes I saw this on an episode of Mad Men!). Fast forward just four decades to dads who car pool, school shop and volunteer for reading time at kindergarten class. Dads who are fully involved in their kids' lives are no longer the exception to the rule, and the growing number of female management and ownership positions has also led to a turning of the tables. The number of stay at home dads has risen sharply in recent years as manual labor jobs have sharply declined. Couples are re-thinking the whole arrangement, and dads staying home with the kids is as good a lane as any other.

This option can open up a lot of family-friendly possibilities for couples since, in many cases, men can re-enter the job market with more ease than women. It might surprise you to learn that men do not seem to handle stay home parenting in the same way that stay home moms do. Stay home dads don't have the "need" to justify their lane choice by overcompensating in other areas. Most stay home moms admit to feeling pressured to keep the house and kids clean and perfect because they have the "luxury" of staying home. Most dads escape such illusions. They are home taking care of the kids, and that is generally what they do. Cleaning the house, grocery shopping, social connections, extended family duties and home maintenance are separate issues to be negotiated in the home of stay home dads.

Unlike other lanes which are coveted by moms (such as working part-time or not working at all), the thought of this lane makes a lot of moms give the proverbial "hell no" at the mention of it. But there are some strong considerations as our culture becomes more compassionate toward dads who want a less work-centered existence and women continue earning more.

First we will go through the pros and the cons of this lane. Then I will give you three solid tips for making this lane work and wrap up with an outline called **Thinking it Through** to help you gauge your reasoning and logic when considering this lane.

The Pros of your spouse staying home:

1. **Paternal care brings its own special brand of influence.** It's no revelation that men parent differently than women and this can be a wonderful influence on your kids. According to the book *Partnership Parenting: How Men and Women Parent Differently by:* Karl Pruett MD & Marsha Pruett PhD (2009), "Men were generally found to be willing to teach children through actions more than through words. Fathers generally allow children to engage in risky behavior (such as climbing the jungle gym alone) in order to develop in them a sense of autonomy, exploration, and tolerance for pain and disappointment."

2. **You get to go to work with peace of mind.** Dads have had this luxury for hundreds of years going to work knowing that their precious families are being cared for by the only other person on the planet who loves their kids as much as they do. For moms that have

time-hogging jobs, this set-up can relieve a lot of worry and concern that usually comes with the critical years (infants, toddlers and teenagers) of your family life.

3. **Men can re-enter the job market after an employment gap infinitely easier than women.** Not only that, they can tell prospective employers exactly what they were doing during their employment gap, and it can actually make them more employable. It's a double standard, and in this case, you can work it to your favor.

4. **Your husband will be part of a growing trend.** There are two million preschoolers whose fathers care for them more hours than any other childcare provider while their mothers are at work. This is a ratio of about one in five preschoolers of employed mothers (The US Census Bureau, 2010).

The Cons of your spouse staying home:

1. **He may like it and never return to work.** This is more common than you think. Most men have been programmed to work work work. Once he's off that treadmill, it is sometimes hard to get him back on. You may have to push to get your hubby to go back to work if the need arises. (Yes, it is a double standard to talk this way because if men said this about stay home moms and work, it would be *war!*).

2. **He will take the job title of childcare literally and will do *only* that.** He is not likely to be home scrubbing floors, handling the social calendar or meal planning while you are at work. So you will have to do it yourself or hire someone to do these things.

3. **Depending on your job, you might get less time with your kids than if you and your spouse were both earning an income.** Face it, forty hours a week is practically part-time in the eyes of most employers, and if you have a "big job" or run your own company you may not get to see your kids enough. This may make you jealous of the time he gets with the kids. Incidentally, this is how men have felt for eons.

4. **He will do it wrong.** Or it may feel that way to you anyway. His parenting style and childcare approach is likely to differ from yours. But if he is the primary childcare provider in your equation, then you will have to concede on some of these items since you cannot be in two places at once. So your second grader goes to school a little dirty, in the too-small clothes that you had in the donation bin, and has a piece of leftover salmon steak fermenting in her lunch box. Everyone will live. Probably.

Three Tips For Making This Lane Work

1. **Get agreement on a list of non-negotiable items when it comes to parenting.** Like don't leave the little kids alone in the car or no provocative clothing allowed for the teenagers. Figure out what will really drive you crazy and make the set-up impossible for you to endure if it's not done your way (you only get a few of these) and then let go. Ultimately you must find a way to trust his parenting style and agree with *most* of his decisions.

2. **Make couple time a priority.** You are in new territory here and this is not the lane to take anyone or anything for granted. You need time to talk and listen to each other and keep communication lines open. It might help to commit to a finite period of time for this career lane and make a list of what each of you can do to support each other fully in this endeavor.

3. **Agree on who does what and don't make assumptions about what "staying home" means.** You can have Hercules at home with your kids, and there will still be lots of items on the to-do list that need to be done. And try not to think in terms of what you would do if you were home—you're not. Put the care of the kids first and go from there with the negotiations.

Thinking It Through

YOU MIGHT WANT TO CONSIDER THIS LANE IF...	YOU MIGHT WANT TO PASS ON THIS LANE IF...	CAUTION SIGNS-SLOW DOWN, CONSIDER OTHER OPTIONS BEFORE PROCEEDING...
It makes logical sense to both of you, and you are both open.	Your husband is going through some deep emotional turmoil and not working anyway.	Think about your own parenting skill on days when you are down or low on sleep. Are you at your best? Is this really what you want for your spouse and your kids? Find an alternative while your husband works through his issues.
Secretly, you feel lucky.	You feel that daycare is wrong, so you are forcing him to stay home because you cannot.	If neither of you want to be home then you should find a way that neither of you stay there. Seriously. You guys are probably smarter than you think—figure something else out.
You are agreeing to do this as a temporary measure, and you are both okay with the unknown aspects of it.	You drew the shorter straw and must go to work.	Jealous mommy counting the hours until she comes home is not a great plan unless it is very short term. Your work/ home set-up should not be a form of hell for you.
In a number of ways he is better equipped to stay home than you are.	The thought of having your husband stay home with your kids gives you a rash or makes you green with envy.	see above.

What do you think about this lane? Do you know anyone who is in this lane? What were your selections in each area? Is this even a remote possibility in your mind?

Notes, thoughts and questions about this lane:

I think every working mom probably feels the same thing: You go through big chunks of time where you're just thinking, 'This is impossible — oh, this is impossible.' And then you just keep going and keep going, and you sort of do the impossible.

-Tina Fey

NOTES:

NOTES:

CHAPTER EIGHT

THE TURNING LANE

You forego income to dedicate time to your education, project, screenplay, novel, etc.

There are now, for the first time in three decades, more young women in school than in the work force. In the last two years, the number of women ages 18 to 24 in school rose by 130,000, compared with a gain of 53,000 for young men.

Imagine for a moment a stay home mother of three in charge of her delightful brood, all under the age of five (no twins) and all cute kids but not great sleepers. During a nap one day, the sleep-deprived mom has vivid and memorable dream of a male vampire and a high school girl laying in a meadow. She wakes and is anxious to follow the story in her mind so she pulls out the family computer and starts to write it down. That mother is *Twilight* author Stephanie Meyer. In interviews Meyer maintains that no one was more surprised than she when she actually finished writing a BOOK. Now her books have sold over 100 million copies in 37 languages. Globally, the *Twilight* films, released in 2008 to 2012 have a $2.4 billion haul at the global box office. Not bad for a stay home mom huh? As someone who has been working on several books for over ten years, I cannot help but wonder: what if she had *not* done it? What if her husband thought it was a stupid, crazy idea (she did not tell him about her writing project initially), or if she did not have the confidence to sustain the effort that went into it? It may be an extreme example, yet it's a completely plausible example at the same time because it did really happen.

Whether it is nursing school, law school, your bachelor's degree, massage certification, art school, or a steamy novel you want to write, this lane is about investing in yourself. It's about taking a chance on your talent and your dream and hope it pays off later. The key with this lane is to logically explore your options and then proceed *without* the need for positive feedback from the outside world, which is easier said than done. This lane is an investment. And like buying stocks, you make your investment and give it time to pay off.

First we will go through the pros and the cons of this lane. Then I will give you three solid tips for making this lane work and wrap up with an outline called **Thinking it Through** to help you gauge your reasoning and logic when considering this lane.

The Pros of working on your project or education or otherwise delaying your return to work:

1. **Finishing your master's degree, becoming an interior designer or finishing that saucy screenplay is a great idea.** Doing what you are really passionate about is a wonderful idea, especially if you have given up work to focus on your kids. It will feel almost like a reward, and it will no doubt be well deserved. Life really is short, and investing time or money to learn is a wonderful use of your resources.

2. **You might get to say 'NO' to work you hate.** Doing work you hate feels especially punishing after having children. So if this plan helps you to never have to do work you hate again, it will add to your life's joy and happiness and your family will benefit from that.

3. **You will have pursued a dream.** Not only is it good for you to feel empowered and creative, it's also good for your kids to see you go after something and make it happen. Lots of people dream it but never do it. You will be among a very small group of people who follow their dreams. As cliché as it sounds, sometimes the outcome is not the goal. Sometimes the journey is what matters.

The Cons of working on your project or education or otherwise delaying your return to work:

1. **You may not finish it.** Stuff happens, and when it does, your passion (which is not likely to be generating income or cleaning your house) will be the first to go on the chopping block. Shelving the project during a summer vacation or even just during a month off from school can turn into years without any progress.

2. **It's hard.** It's hard to justify it to your spouse and even to yourself. One or both of you will have issues with the investment of money or time or both at some point in the process. There is pressure to comply with the black-and-white, work-or-not-work model, and this is like a grey area. You will feel pressure from the outside as well as from yourself.

3. **You might be pursuing the wrong thing for you and end up hating it.** Nursing school is a great example of this. Because there are jobs available in the nursing field, suddenly lots of women with career angst are considering nursing school, whether or not it would be a good fit. This is not a good reason to choose a path to follow. And if you choose something out of guilt or logic then you might be investing years in something you don't really want to do.

4. **People might treat you like a slacker.** You might feel a bit awkward in social situations because people (especially in the US) tend to have more positive associations with work, keeping busy and even being overwhelmed than with studying, creating, or developing an idea. But they will be secretly jealous so don't let it get to you.

Three Tips To Making This Lane Work

1. **Get your spouse's buy-in initially, but teach yourself to not need it later.** Obviously this is a team decision. So you will want to be clear, do the math, and really figure out how it might work over the period of time you need to accomplish your goals. After that,

look elsewhere for encouragement and the strength to carry on. It is likely that no one will be more inconvenienced by your project than your spouse. So it's a bit much to expect him to be your cheering squad all the time as well.

2. **Set deadlines and goals.** Having a plan and deadlines is critical to your success but making them realistic and attainable is even more important. Don't tell yourself that you will write ten chapters in the next four days because not attaining it will impact your self-esteem and you will need lots of self-esteem to finish your project. The old adage about setting goals (S.M.A.R.T.) still holds true: setting specific, measurable, achievable, realistic goals with a timeline will be very helpful.

3. **Commit.** Send the check, register for the class, set up the blog—whatever that action step is that makes you committed to the project needs to be done. Once you commit, commit not to quit. Like that great quote, "Commitment is continuing to do something long after the mood has left you." You will need to guard your dreams and plans against the inevitability of life.

Thinking It Through

YOU MIGHT WANT TO CONSIDER THIS LANE IF...	YOU MIGHT WANT TO PASS ON THIS LANE IF...	CAUTION SIGNS-SLOW DOWN, CONSIDER OTHER OPTIONS BEFORE PROCEEDING...
This dream of yours pesters you and you cannot make the idea of it go away (this very book is an example of a dream that pestered me relentlessly until I finished it!).	You are doing it as a cover for wanting to stay home with your kids.	If you want to stay home with your kids and it makes sense (See Chapter Three: *The Center Lane*) then find a way to do it. You don't have to come up with some kind of cover story to justify it.

The funding is somehow available or reasonable, and it makes as much sense now as it ever will.	You are confused about what to do so you are toying with this project for now.	Devoting yourself to a project that does not pay (yet) has within it the capacity to boost or crush your self-esteem. If you are confused, then find a way to get clear before you start this project because embarking on it and not making progress has the capacity to do more harm than good.
The funding is not really there but it won't make your family homeless to do it either.	You know you will never finish or accomplish this project.	Creative work or adult education is not for the faint at heart. Dig deep and make sure this is something you truly want to finish before you start.

Is there something you have always wanted to do that would require a block of time or additional schooling? Whose career or accomplishments do you envy the most? What has your spouse always wanted to do?

Notes, thoughts and questions about this lane:

Believe in something larger than yourself... get involved in the big ideas of your time.

-Barbara Bush

NOTES:

CHAPTER NINE

THE MERGE LANE

You both work part-time while sharing childcare and home management equally.

According to FlexJobs CEO, Sara Sutton Fell, job listings at the online professional job service company for flexible positions has grown by 400%, with listings in more than fifty career fields, entry-level to executive, part-time to full-time.

The thought of this lane conjures up one word for me: envy. It's actually a genius idea to have a couple who both work part-time and parent equally. This lane addresses the downsides of the mom working part-time: her doing so much more at home than her full-time working spouse and condensing her schedule at work so she is cramming in full-time work for part-time pay. While this lane gets little use currently, it could become a growing trend.

Clearly this lane requires some special circumstances at work as well as uncertainty regarding health insurance and other benefits. But if one of you works at Starbucks and the other in the health care profession or a job share role, it can be ideal to work part of the week and then divide duties at home and with the kids. If something changes and one employer requires full-time, one lane will have to change. But both temporarily and long term, this can be a great lane.

First we will go through the pros and the cons of this lane. Then I will give you three solid tips for making this lane work and wrap up with an outline called Thinking it Through to help you gauge your reasoning and logic when considering this lane.

The Pros of both working part-time and parenting equally:

1. **Your husband will "get" you.** This arrangement will likely help your spouse relate to you in a way that is atypical unless he has been a single parent or widowed in the past. Now he will "get it" in a way that perhaps he never did before. Bonus side effect: this will make you WANT him.

2. **You each get the best of both worlds and your kids will benefit from the fairness and gender equality in the home.** Heck, yeah! Norwegians have nothing on your family. You are trendy, cool and way ahead of your time. This team approach could encourage kids to contribute and do "their part" with less argument.

3. **Neither of you has to be the over-worked part of your team.** What a concept to have things as fair and balanced as they can be when it comes to the full-meal-deal that is parenting. If one of you used to work seventy plus hours per week and never saw the kids, this set-up can be a dream come true because you both work and both contribute to parenting and domestic life.

The Cons of both working part-time and parenting equally:

1. **Healthcare and benefits might become an issue.** Who knows where the whole health care system is going? Full-time work might become necessary so that you can receive employer paid healthcare. Depending how long you stay in this lane, you will likely earn fewer benefits like 401K and stock options than you would working full-time. This could impact your retirement and long- term finances.

2. **You will have to share decisions with him that you might otherwise just make on your own.** Equality is equality, and the concept can prove frustrating to some. You might be used to taking the primary caregiver role where you get to be the boss of things for the

most part (even though you complain about it) and this would no longer be the case if you are sharing equally.

3. **Everything becomes a negotiation.** Couples can take this concept too far and negotiate the little kindnesses and romance right out of the equation by splitting everything 50/50. Not very romantic.

4. **People may look down on you or even think your husband is a sissy.** You might have to get some new friends.

5. **You might risk future promotions at work.** The same risks apply here if only one of you works part-time, except that the risk affects both of you. If you are both self employed, it might be a non-issue.

Three Tips For Making This Lane Work

1. **Divide by responsibility preferences first — then equity.** Sit down and communicate with each other what areas of responsibility you love and hate. There is a chance you love what your spouse hates and vice-versa. For the remaining items, you can negotiate. It's silly to just take turns doing everything. If you hate driving and he doesn't mind it, put it on his half of the list.

2. **Agree that the sharing of tasks may be 60/40.** Trying to set things up as a 50/50 split leaves no room for special skills and preferences, and it is just too structured.

3. **The one who earns more income does not do less work at home.** It will never work this way. You are agreeing to do this based on a desire for life balance and equal parenting. Part-time work and part-time parenting is just that and who earns more should not really play into the equation. You cannot work a little more or a little less at home based on your income. That would be simply mixing old traditions with a new concept, which defeats the purpose.

Thinking It Through

YOU MIGHT WANT TO CONSIDER THIS LANE IF...	YOU MIGHT WANT TO PASS ON THIS LANE IF...	CAUTION SIGNS-SLOW DOWN, CONSIDER OTHER OPTIONS BEFORE PROCEEDING...
You both really want to do it, and you have the opportunity to do it without permanent harm to your career/s.	It makes no sense financially but you both want to do it.	It's hard not to be impulsive when it comes to decisions that affect our kids and family. Try to really think it through before you both go part-time. There may be alternatives that work just as well without the career risk and loss of income.
You are just that kind of cutting-edge couple and you see it as a social experiment.	Neither of you will have any foreseeable life outside of your work and your children if you do this.	Your relationship is a critical part of the parenting equation. Try to come up with a plan that will not turn your spouse into your co-worker or boss.
You are non-traditional in many aspects and this plan is consistent with your approach to other aspects of marriage, income earning and parenting.	You are competitive with each other and there is no way you are going to work full-time while letting your spouse get more time with the kids.	Lots of couples are competitive with each other. Although it is common, it is not benign and nothing about being in competition with each other is a good idea for your kids. You have other issues—work them out some more before trying this lane.

Is this possible for you and your spouse? What would it look like? If your spouse worked part-time, what might that look like? What about benefits? Is this a future goal?

Notes, thoughts and questions about this lane:

*My life comes down to three moments: the death of my father,
meeting my husband, and the birth of my daughter. Everything I did
previous to that just doesn't seem to add up to very much.*

-Gwyneth Paltrow

NOTES:

PART III

RESETTING YOUR GPS

TOOLS FOR AWARENESS

Who in the world am I? Ah, that's the great puzzle.
-Lewis Carroll, Alice in Wonderland

Welcome to the TOOLS chapter of *What's Your Lane*? The exercises in this chapter will help you understand your decisions, and more importantly, what is behind your decisions and dominant beliefs. Understanding what we truly believe and desire for our family and for ourselves gives us tremendous power, because from that platform of knowing ourselves, we can take action that makes sense of our lives.

The most powerful outcome in my coaching practice is when a client tells me they have a new sense of clarity and direction on a formerly stubborn, complicated issue. While I get a thrill from playing a part in that realization, I am not being humble at all when I say it was there all along. My job as a coach is to simply create the space for the person to hear themselves think. The most powerful way to create the space is to ask questions and listen intently to the answers. That is what coaches do. The exercises in this chapter are meant to create that space for you. You can do the exercises as they are assigned in the book chapters, or you can do them all at once. You can find extra, blank copies of the exercises at my website: www.WhatsYourLane.com if you want them in PDF format for multiple uses. So go ahead and write in this book or grab a journal if you are reading on an electronic device.

The Power Of A Question

Writing a book with questions and "work" is not the most popular approach to take. Generally speaking, people like to read and do not always want to be bothered with exercises. Publishers and editors agree, because providing a space for people to write is untidy and does not fit the mold of most books. But I always knew this book would have coaching exercises in it for the reader, because motherhood is so fraught with noise from everyone else's thoughts that we need a place to process our own. I also knew that this book would have *work* because I can say with complete honesty that some of the books I have read literally changed the course of my life. In the acknowledgement section of this book, I thank many of the authors who published books that caused me to "do the work" by writing down the answers to questions in their books. Authors like Tony Robbins, Martha Beck, Harriett Klauser and Julia Cameron impacted my business, my relationships, and my life path.

One of the most powerful books for me was *New York Times* bestseller <u>Keeping the Love You Find</u> by Harville Hendrix, which I read nearly twenty years ago (I still buy the book for newlyweds and for people struggling with relationship issues). It must have taken me eight months to get through his book. I recall answering the questions in my own shorthand code in case someone happened upon my book and saw my answers to his questions about childhood wounds and other sensitive subjects. I answered the questions because I was lonely and really ready to stop having bad relationships with the wrong people, but I was doing so without much result or outcome at the time. Truth be told, I hated Harville Hendrix for eight months. It was on the last few pages of the book when I had a realization about my repeated pattern with relationships that was so obvious that it made me laugh out loud. Suddenly all of the "stupid" personal questions I had answered clicked in a way that helped me understand why history kept repeating itself. From that moment I could recognize the "wrong guy" on the first date instead of investing years in a bad relationship, and that ability transformed my life. All that because I wrote my honest answers to questions in a book! Let's be clear, I am no Dr. Harville Hendrix, but I have some game in this realm of self-discovery, so stick with me and do the exercises. Like most good things, self-discovery is a process and usually has layers. Let's start peeling away.

COACHING ASSIGNMENT #1   10 MINUTES
Beginning Assessment-Where Am I Now?

In coaching we always start with where we are now. You can set aside explanations and blame and justifications and just write about where you currently "reside" when it comes to work and career. There are no conclusion or results sections to this exercise. You are simply writing about your current set-up. When finished, continue to Chapter One: Checking Under the Hood.

(Don't over-think or analyze – just write. This is an individual exercise – not a couples' thing).

1. List at least three things that you <u>love</u> about your current situation or set-up as it relates to <u>work</u> and <u>family</u>:

....

....

....

2. List at least three things you <u>don't like</u> about your current situation:

....

....

....

3. What work/family arrangement do you think your partner, if you currently have one, would choose for you if he/she could? (Don't worry, it is not their choice, but do answer the question!)

....

....

....

Complete the following sentences:
1. When it comes to my <u>current</u> situation, what I fear or worry most about is:

....

....

2. When I even try to imagine other possibilities for myself I fear or worry about:

_____

_____

3. If money were not an issue, and I knew that my children would grow up to be well adjusted and happy adults regardless of my occupation or creative adventures, I would _____

_____ for a living.

4. Doing the (above) for a living would be appealing to me because :

_____

_____

5. Think back to a time when everything seemed to "work" well in your household—even if it was for an hour, a day or a week. Consider your relationships, your satisfaction as a parent, work, finances, etc. What elements created that formula (even if the time was only two weeks long, or it was on vacation, or before your fourth child was born)? Describe what was going on, what worked, and what elements were in place:

_____

_____

_____

_____

_____

_____

A mother is not a person to lean on, but a person to make leaning unnecessary.

-Dorothy Canfield Fisher

COACHING ASSIGNMENT #2   10-15 MINUTES
Parenting Beliefs Exercise

I designed this easy exercise to help you become aware of your beliefs and discover the life experiences that had a hand in shaping them. Once you know which beliefs and experiences shaped your decisions, you can decide to keep them or quiet them and give them more or less power in your life. We're not trying to change or alter beliefs here, just to become aware of them. Our goal is to have the beliefxs come out of the dark where we can notice and possibly examine them. There are no trick questions and there are no wrong answers — it's just an exercise.

Circle the <u>three</u>, most accurate descriptions of <u>your</u> personal parenting style below:

Fun Mamma	The Hammer	Cuddly Bear
Adventure Mom	Protective Lioness	Hottie Mommy
Safety Mom	Enabler Mom	Fitness Mom
Lecture Mom	Modern Mom	Crafty Mom
Reluctant Mom	Party Mom	Poetic Mom
Rock Mamma	Perfect Mom	Relaxed Mommy
Righteous Mom	European Mom	Empowerment Mom
Celebrity Mom	Granola Mom	Spiritual Mom
Militant Mom	Intermittent Mom	Controlling Mother
Cool Mom	Cerebral Mamma	Mother Earth Goddess
Hardworking Mom	Cheerleader Mom	Unavailable Mom

Now, to discover how you developed the identities above, fill in the blanks below:

  1. I circled _____, _____ and

  _____.

2. If I had to pick one description of me that I am most <u>proud</u> of it would be _____.

3. The reason I am that way (from number two above) is probably be-cause of my life experience of _____

_____

_____

_____

_____

_____

4. If I had to pick one of my identities that I am *least* proud of (out of my three choices) that would have to be_____

_____.

5. I think this parenting style (from number four above) serves me in a positive way because _____

_____

_____

6. I think this parenting style (from number four above) could also have a negative effect and that would have to be _____

_____

_____

7. Continue pondering how your life experiences and the beliefs they have created shape your parenting style and choices and write notes and observations below:

_____

_____

_____

_____

_____

_____

_____

_____

_____

_____

Our deepest fear is not that we are inadequate. Our deepest fear is that we are powerful beyond measure. It is our Light, not our Darkness, that most frightens us.

-Marianne Williamson

COACHING ASSIGNMENT #3   10 MINUTES
My Unique Judgments

Below is a quick and easy way to unearth some of your more overt parenting judgments and use them to uncover the beliefs or experiences they might be associated with. The easiest way to do this is to imagine that you are in a busy shopping mall play area or amusement park viewing other mothers and their children. And yes, for the sake of this exercise, it is good to be judgmental. Like the previous two exercises, this is just a building and uncovering process. No conclusions yet.

Fill in the blanks below:

1. Good mothers tend to be _____
   _____ with their children and are
   almost always_____.

2. I can tell a good mother by the way she_____
   _____, and similarly I take a lot of pride in the
   way I_____.

3. It irritates me when I see parents _____
   _____their children because
   I feel this is not appropriate or right.

4. If I were the Supreme Ruler of Parenting Advice I would make
   every parent _____ and _____
   _____with their children.

Reflection

Now re-read your answers and see if you can see some common threads within your judgments. Jot down any observations _____

_____

_____

_____

_____

_____.

Fill in the blanks below:

5. If I could change one thing about **my own** parenting habits I would
_____a lot <u>less</u> and _____
_____ a lot <u>more</u>.

6. This is (positive quality from number five above) important to me because

_____

_____

_____

_____.

7. When I think back on my upbringing, I am **embarrassed** about
_____and _____
_____.

8. When I think back on my upbringing, I am most **proud** of _____
_____and_____
_____
_____.

9. Write a little bit about what you find is the most **relevant discovery** from the information above especially as it relates to your current parenting choices and judgments. (Is it that your judgments come from certain life experiences? Are the most embarrassing aspects of your childhood impacting your parenting now?)

_____

_____

_____

_____

_____

_____

_____

_____

_____

_____

_____

_____

_____

_____.

Where there is no struggle, there is no strength.
-Oprah Winfrey

COACHING ASSIGNMENT #4   20 MINUTES
The Going to the Ugly

Do you need a mental health professional? If you are having thoughts of harming yourself or others get yourself the help you need. Seriously, this exercise is not a substitute for therapy or for working with a licensed mental health professional.

Welcome to a process that I use with my coaching clients when they are stressed to the point of being stuck. I also use it myself from time to time. GTTU is a favorite of top-level executives, team leaders, account reps and job seekers alike. *Going to the Ugly* is about opening the "container" that you do NOT want to open. The idea is to "go there" in order to air things out and make better decisions and arrive at some clarity — all things that are nearly impossible to attain without examination. GTTU may seem a bit counter intuitive because our social programming tells us that we should strive to stay positive. But in order to authentically go from negative to positive there is a critical, important step — especially if you are feeling like your current situation seems unsustainable.

One way to look at this process is to imagine that the *inner you* wants the *outer you* to get some stuff off your chest so that you can find the "prize inside." There are three simple steps to doing this, but first you must pick something that you are currently unhappy with. It helps if it is a situation (vs. a person) but it will work if you have a person in mind as well. Picking something real and relevant in your life currently will help you to learn the process and derive the most benefit. Don't put it off until later — do it right now.

So pick something, and then read the three steps. Next we will break each one down. I have also included a complete sample of a real-life *Going to the Ugly* situation. But don't read any more until you come up with your situation: anything that you are *intensely dissatisfied* with.

Sample ideas of dissatisfaction:

I hate everything my husband does.

I do everything around here and I am sick of it.

I hate my job and cannot stand Melissa, the new manager.

My in-laws are obnoxious and butt into our lives.

My kids are brats.

I am exhausted to the core of my being—all of the time.

We are broke and might lose our home.

The 3 Basic Steps of the *Going To The Ugly* Strategy:

1. **Complain.** In the space provided you will encourage yourself to complain—this is an essential part of *Going to the Ugly*. There are some prompts to help you complain more.

A full page is provided but go further if you can.

2. **Review your complaints and answer some questions about them. See what else comes up.**
3. **Brainstorm with yourself and commit to a temporary conclusion based on your findings.**

Sample of the complete GTTU Process:

Here is an example that you can read through to help you prime the pump. But NO value can be had from just reading. You must write your own stuff to get the benefit from *Going to the Ugly*.

Example:

Step 1 – Going to the Ugly.

Take as many words as you need to describe a situation that is unsustainable to you:

I am the sole caregiver for my father, who has early Alzheimer's, and I have two kids and a house; I cannot deal with it anymore, but I am stuck – I have no out. I am exhausted and sick of it and I am just completely stuck. It could be years before he dies and the kids need me and I am just fed up beyond words. My life is nothing like I thought it would be. I feel like I am failing on every level, and I do not even know who I am right now.

If I had a magic wand:

Some angel would appear who could care for Dad, and I would not have to go to his place three times per day. I am so exhausted that I don't even know who I am anymore.

The truth that I cannot say to anyone is:

It sucks that I am stuck taking care of him. He does not even recognize me. I was already slammed, and I feel like I am going to die of exhaustion. The situation is impossible, and it is making me hate my life.

The worst part is:

I feel like I am neglecting my kids to take care of him. It's not fair. I don't deserve this. And it's ironic since he paid no attention to me whatsoever when I was growing up. And what about my siblings, Mel and George? How do they sleep at night? They are his kids too, but because they live far away, they don't have to deal with it.

I have tried to resolve this by:

I have tried to hint to my siblings that I need help, but they are busy too, and nothing has changed. I feel stuck, and it is making me hate my life.

Step 2 – Review your complaints and answer some questions about them. See what else comes up.

Go back and re-read what you have read with some distance. Pretend you are someone else reading about you. Write compassionately about what you have read. When I go back and re-read my writing, I see that I am taking everything on myself. It is clear that it is not fair. I resent the fact that my parents did not make better arrangements for themselves, but that ship has sailed; Mom is gone and Dad is not "Dad" anymore. It sucks. I have always wondered what would happen if my husband Burt's parents got ill. Would he expect me to take care of them too? He expects me to handle everything while he just goes about his business. What kind *of husband lets his wife get up in the middle of the night and drive across town to check on her dad all by herself?*

The truth of the matter is:

I take great care of my husband's parents and our kids, and he's not supporting me. He's making life harder by not doing anything extra around here for our kids. Who does that? Maybe that is really what is going on with me. It feels like it's more about my husband than my dad.

Step 3 – Brainstorm with yourself and commit to temporary conclusion.

So I guess I am really mad at Burt. Wow, didn't see that one coming. I can tell that I hit on something though, because the knot in my stomach feels looser. I am still stuck, but at least I know why I am angry now.

Conclusion: List some random ideas for making progress on this item

Some random ideas for addressing this are:

-Talk to Burt about my feelings and ask him how he would feel if it was his dad and I was not helpful or at all supportive enough.
-Call my sister and tell her that I either need money or time from her and George. It is that simple; I cannot continue on this path indefinitely.
-Put my foot down with the kids and their messy habits. I am sick of picking up the same stuff over and over. They are old enough to pick up after themselves.

> *The truth is that our finest moments are most likely to occur when we are feeling deeply uncomfortable, unhappy, or unfulfilled. For it is only in such moments, propelled by our discomfort, that we are likely to step out of our ruts and start searching for different ways or truer answers.*
> *-M. Scott Peck*

Your Turn to *Go to the Ugly*

Think of something that is really bugging you about your life or a person in your life — or everything in your life.

Step 1 - **Encourage more complaints.** This is a private writing. You do not have to share this or express it to anyone but yourself. Use a list form or write a paragraph or two, or a few pages. Just write, uncensored, without thought for grammar or spelling. For my clients I set a timer (five minutes if they are saying it to me and ten if they are writing it on their own). Use shorthand or code for names if you like — but write. Be brutal, blunt and absolutely *un-Christianlike*.

The Buddha and other spiritual teachers tell us that when we have troubles, we should "lean into them," which sounds much nicer than complaining. But the advice is the same: dig deeper into your unhappiness. And don't worry that it will never stop — it will. I promise.

Step 1: Take as many words as you need to describe a situation that is unsustainable to you:

_____

_____

_____

_____

_____

_____

_____

_____

_____

_____

Prompts provided in spaces below to help you complain further...

If I had a magic wand:

_____

_____

_____

_____

_____

_____

_____

_____

_____

_____

The truth that I cannot say to anyone is:

_____

_____

_____

_____

_____

_____

_____

_____

_____

_____

The worst part is:

_____

_____

_____

_____

_____

_____

_____

_____

_____

_____

I have tried to resolve this by:

_____

_____

_____

_____

_____

_____

_____

_____

_____

_____

Okay, if you did this correctly you should be feeling pretty bad right now.

Step 2 – Re-read and review your complaints above and answer some questions below about what you wrote to see what else comes up. The thing that is really bothering you is almost never the thing that started you down this path, and it is very important that you uncover what is underneath. We humans are a complicated bunch. Often what starts as one feeling ends up being something else entirely. Dig a little deeper and keep asking. Trust me, when you stumble upon what you are really feeling, *you will know it because it will feel relieving to know what is really bothering you.* Until that time, keep digging.

Take a breath and then go back and re-read what you have read with some distance. Pretend you are someone else reading about you.

Write compassionately about what you have read:

_____

_____

_____

_____

_____

_____

_____

_____

_____

_____

_____

The truth of the matter is:

_____

_____

_____

_____

_____

_____

_____

_____

_____

_____

Step 3 – Brainstorm with yourself and commit to a temporary conclusion. Going to the Ugly is a good practice and digging deeper is good as well, but you are not allowed to stay there. If you stay there, you will be a confused, emotional mess, and nobody wants that. Instead, give yourself a day or two to process what you came up with, but right now come up with some temporary conclusions about your feelings. You do not *have to* take action, although your brain may give you valuable ideas and you might choose to act on them. The main point is to come up with some conclusions about your true feelings. Learning to recognize how we really feel is a talent and mastering it can come in very handy if you want clearer direction in your life.

Answer the following questions and then make a temporary conclusion and list some possible ideas.

What I am really feeling is:

_____

_____

_____

_____

_____

_____

_____

_____

_____

_____

That is interesting because:

_____

_____

_____

_____

_____

_____

_____

_____

_____

_____

I can tell that I hit on something real because:

_____

_____

_____

_____

_____

_____

_____

_____

_____

_____

If I decide to take action based on this discovery, some random,

undeveloped ideas might include:

_____

_____

_____

_____

_____

_____

_____

_____

_____

Good job. My clients often say they feel a shift or a sense of clarity about the issue that seemed impossible just twenty minutes ago. The goal is not to solve the problem or issue but to get some clarity so that we can put the best part of ourselves to work on the issue. And just to be clear, it's not that the issue was all in your head. On the contrary, often our biggest issues have to do with other people in our lives and those people might actually be culpable. The reason the exercise works is that it helps us scrape away some of the build-up of stress that makes the situation look impossible. We cannot make any real progress until we admit all of the ugly truth from our perspective. After all, ours is the only perspective that really matters currently since we are the angry or frustrated person at the moment. Often, within a moment of clarity, we can come up with a game plan that is useful. If instead you find that you are still frustrated after completing the exercise, go back and re-read your work, and then just let it go. Give it a few days to incubate.

For the next few weeks, notice when you feel angry. While a reaction to someone or something often starts with feeling angry, examine it further and see if you notice what is underneath the anger. Often just beneath the anger is something more in the realm of disappointment for example. Disappointment implies that we have unmet expectations and it can be helpful to admit that we are disappointed vs. just mad. Give it some thought the next time a strong emotion crops up by settling into it a bit and seeing what else it might lead to. As for *Going to the Ugly,* you can use your journal or just pound away at the keyboard — but go there.

Healing yourself is connected with healing others.
                                              -Yoko Ono

COACHING ASSIGNMENT #5   30 MINUTES
The Division of Labor in Your Home – Assessment and related reading

If you are like most moms you often feel exhausted, overworked and overwrought, and things at home feel downright unfair from your perspective. At least part of the reason you feel overwhelmed is the concept we discussed in Chapter One. The "life" we share with our spouses and our offspring tends to take on a life of its own. You probably give yourself credit for parenting, for maintaining your relationship and maintaining your health (well somewhat anyway). But there is a whole container of life-stuff that you are probably not even aware that you do. This assessment is a way of putting it on paper so that you can look at it. This is a glimpse, a quick exploration, to help you understand and appreciate all that gets done in your life.

Instructions: Give each task a rating of 1 or 0 in each column. You may split the 1 over two columns, giving each a rating of .5. If you do part of a task and your partner does part, just split it 50/50. If someone else also helps, split it that way, but it is not necessary to split beyond a rating of .5 to glean the full benefit from this assessment. Don't over-think or over-complicate and definitely don't put it into a spreadsheet and write an algorithm for it. Just run through the list in 15 minutes or less plus scoring time. Like all of the exercises in this book, and journaling, it is best for you to do this alone.

> *Divide and conquer.*
> *-Philip II, King of Macedon (382-336 BC)*

DIVISION OF LABOR

HOUSEHOLD/OUTDOORS:	I DO	HE DOES	SOMEONE ELSE DOES	NOT RELEVANT
Patio or Porch Area				
Garbage/recycling				
Flowers				
Trees/shrubbery				
Grass/landscaping				
Garage organization and maintenance				
SUBTOTAL:	/6	/6	/6	/6

SOCIAL:	I DO	HE DOES	SOMEONE ELSE DOES	NOT RELEVANT
Invitations to friends and family				
Accepting/declining invites				
Birthday gifts/holiday gifts: kids				
Birthday gifts/holiday gifts: extended family				
Shipping/post office/related errands				
Prep house for entertaining guests				
Cooking for guests				
Communicating with world on behalf of family/social media				
SUBTOTAL:	/8	/8	/8	/8

HOUSEWORK:	I DO	HE DOES	SOMEONE ELSE DOES	NOT RELEVANT
Dishes				
Appliances cleaning (refrigerator/oven/stove, etc.)				
Vacuuming				
Dusting				
Snow removal/weather related work				
Bathrooms				

Windows				
Window coverings				
Floors				
Your room				
Kids' rooms				
Family room				
Basement				
Living room				
SUBTOTAL:	/14	/14	/14	/14

MAINTENANCE:	I DO	HE DOES	SOMEONE ELSE DOES	NOT RELEVANT
Fixes or calls and arranges repair				
Stays with repair person				
Obtains bids, researches prices, shops etc.				
SUBTOTAL:	/3	/3	/3	/3

HIRED HELPERS— WHO MANAGES THIS RELATIONSHIP?	I DO	HE DOES	SOMEONE ELSE DOES	NOT RELEVANT
Cleaning person/crew				
Gardening/landscaping				
Childcare/babysitters				
Mother's Helpers				
Pool				
Snow removal				
SUBTOTAL:	/6	/6	/6	/6

LAUNDRY:	I DO	HE DOES	SOMEONE ELSE DOES	NOT RELEVANT
Clothes washing				
Folding/put away				
Ironing				
Dry cleaning				
SUBTOTAL:	/4	/4	/4	/4

FOOD:	I DO	HE DOES	SOMEONE ELSE DOES	NOT RELEVANT
Grocery shopping				
Grocery unloading and food storage				
Family breakfast				
Family lunch				
Family dinner				
School lunch packing				
Meal planning				
SUBTOTAL:	/7	/7	/7	/7

FAMILY VACATIONS/ OUTINGS:	I DO	HE DOES	SOMEONE ELSE DOES	NOT RELEVANT
Airlines/Car/Hotel Reservations				
Camera equipment/photo and video taking/post production work				
Route/Point A to Point B				
Vacation/outing planner				
House shut down/house or pet sitters, etc.				
Packing suitcases/food/ medications				
Loading up car/camper/ parking permits etc.				
SUBTOTAL:	/7	/7	/7	/7

MEDICAL CARE:	I DO	HE DOES	SOMEONE ELSE DOES	NOT RELEVANT
Your care – scheduling, inc.				
His care – scheduling, inc.				
Child(ren)pediatrician- scheduling, researching, prescriptions, etc.				
Dental				
Pets				
Elder care				
SUBTOTAL:	/6	/6	/6	/6

HOLIDAYS:	I DO	HE DOES	SOMEONE ELSE DOES	NOT RELEVANT
Decorations outside				
Decorations inside				
Special related rituals like Passover, egg decorating, costumes, etc.				
Shopping - Food				
Shopping - Gifts				
SUBTOTAL:	/5	/5	/5	/5

MONEY:	I DO	HE DOES	SOMEONE ELSE DOES	NOT RELEVANT
Pays bills				
Banking/balancing/juggling, etc.				
Forecasting for future/budgeting/working with financial planner, etc.				
Mortgage/rent/related and managing "portfolio"				
SUBTOTAL:	/4	/4	/4	/4

AUTOMOBILES:	I DO	HE DOES	SOMEONE ELSE DOES	NOT RELEVANT
Car 1 scheduled maintenance				
Car 2 scheduled maintenance				
Gas and washing				
Breakdowns/Problems				
SUBTOTAL:	/4	/4	/4	/4

CHILD MINDING:	I DO	HE DOES	SOMEONE ELSE DOES	NOT RELEVANT
Wake up kids (then wake up again)				
Daytime with kids (non-school age)				
Pick up kids				
Drop off kids				
Parenting: teaching skills for independence				
Parenting: discipline				
SUBTOTAL:	/6	/6	/6	/6

SCHOOL MANAGEMENT:	I DO	HE DOES	SOMEONE ELSE DOES	NOT RELEVANT
Paperwork incoming/ outgoing including homework				
Coordinate schedule(s)				
School events, concerts, rehearsals, details and permissions				
Volunteering/Activism				
Parent/ teacher interaction				
Special needs handling				
SUBTOTAL:	/6	/6	/6	/6

SUMMARY & GRAND TOTALS:	I DO	HE DOES	SOMEONE ELSE DOES	NOT RELEVANT
Household/Outdoors:	/6	/6	/6	/6
Social:	/8	/8	/8	/8
Housework:	/14	/14	/14	/14
Maintenance:	/3	/3	/3	/3
Helpers—Who manages this relationship?	/6	/6	/6	/6
Laundry:	/4	/4	/4	/4
Food:	/7	/7	/7	/7
Family Vacations :	/7	/7	/7	/7
Medical Care:	/6	/6	/6	/6
Holidays:	/5	/5	/5	/5
Money:	/4	/4	/4	/4
Automobiles:	/4	/4	/4	/4
Child Minding:	/6	/6	/6	/6
School Management:	/6	/6	/6	/6
GRAND TOTAL:	/86	/86	/86	/86

Great! So Now What?

It is important to remember that your scores are not good or bad, right or wrong. They simply give a glimpse of your current division of labor. The score does not take into consideration the dynamics between you and your spouse and the things that happened to get you where you are. But we know that those details matter. Perhaps you used to hire out a large part of this list to house helpers until your partner lost his job and your biggest client downsized you to half time. So now things are a bit lopsided, but you are making do. Great! The point here is not to use this as a tool to bash yourself *or your partner*. Instead, just sit with it awhile.

Rethinking Your Math

You may notice that the assessment does not weigh certain jobs as more important than others. This is done deliberately to keep people from arguing a case that could never be fairly decided. For example, how would you weigh getting the kids ready for school each morning against selling your car on Craigslist? Or doing homework with kids every night against moving your grandma into a nursing home? Trying to weigh importance would create a world war between spouses because it is completely subjective and because the level of complication can vary dramatically. But you might want to look at the list and re-think things if you are feeling overwhelmed or hopeless about the long-term possibility of sustaining *your* workload. For example, if you are a stay home mom and have one child, but you have a housekeeper clean your home weekly, many people would say you are one lucky girl. You might think, "My gosh, I only have one kid, my husband works full-time, and he cuts the lawn and takes out the garbage. Jeez, what more do I want?" But look again at the assessment scores. The housekeeper is great, but now it is clear on paper that house-keeping covers only a small portion of the tasks in the grand to-do list of your lives, and there is still a lot to do. In most cases it is simply too much for one person.

Your Preferences and Grievances Matter

Take a look at your totals and also give some thought to how each fits with you, your spouse *and* your dynamic with each other. Really, I prom-ise this is more important than the actual scores. For example, most of the effort for meals in our home is on my side. I really don't mind this. I actually prefer it. But one thing I really used to resent was handling maintenance and repair visits. I work from home and my husband used to schedule things like dishwasher repair, a garage door replacement, plumbing, etc. Then he would go off to work, leaving me to deal with the repair person. I resented this because I would have to interrupt my work to let the repair person in and inevitably they would have a number of questions that I could not answer. I would have to call my husband and he would end up talking to the repair guy on the phone and answering a bunch of questions specific to the task while I stood there like the "silly little wife" who knows nothing about plumbing or underground, decommissioned water heaters. I hated this routine so much that I actually find myself getting annoyed right now just writing about it! Finally, a few years ago, I sat my husband down and explained my frustration with this habit we had developed. He was completely surprised. We talked it out, and now he schedules repairs on days when he can go into work a little later or run home early so he can be present for the repair people. What's funny is that he actually seems to enjoy it. He gets into it. It took us about ten years (and a lot of resentment on my side) to figure that one out.

Splitting the list down the middle and holding each other accountable for the tasks is not the goal of this exercise. Look more closely and see what can change without too much fanfare—and change it. Maybe in the end, your partner cannot change a thing but you get to feel heard and can ask for certain trade-offs that make sustaining your set-up more humane. One mom I know literally does everything for her husband and three kids. Her husband is an executive and they have their deal worked out amazingly well. She has found and purchased all three of their homes, two included a move to a different state. She paints rooms, fixes things, volunteers at school, tends to every aspect of the kids, cooks, cleans (with a little help from a housekeeper thank goodness) and plans family vacations down to the packing of her husband's suitcase and picking him up at work on the way to airport. She says, "Yep, the only thing he does that I don't is earn money and pee standing up." But every Sunday she is "OFF." She sleeps late, reads in bed, works out for two hours and snuggles with her kids and husband, but he handles everything else. For the past seven years, her husband has used one week of his vacation to stay home while she goes to a spa with her mother or a girlfriend. That is their program, and for now it works for them. If she resented it or felt that she gave up too much in the equation then it would not be worth the trade-offs for keeping it the same.

Rehab For Perfectionists

I know what many of you are thinking: "Sure, I do too much, but I am very selective about how I like things done, so I do them myself." So many women say things like, "I could never let him load the dishwasher, wash my clothes or put the kids to bed." This always cracks me up. The last time I checked, men were running the world. I mean really, with a few notable exceptions, the entire planet is run by men. So the next time you think you have to do it yourself because he won't do it right, say to yourself, "If men can run the world, they can load the dishwasher." You may have two or three things that you simply cannot delegate or let go of. That is fine. But if you have fifteen or twenty things that absolutely must be done your way, then you probably need to do some work in this area. You might even need some therapy. No kidding; those domestic perfection genes run deep and many of us have "issues" with letting people help us. Plus, you might be a bitch to live with because of your perfectionism. Really, is that what you want? So take a deep breath and give it some thought. Go back over the assessment and put a star next to items you *might* be willing to let someone else do.

Who Died And Left You In Charge Of Everything?

My husband and I have a friend who is a corporate psychologist. Ben is married but does not have children. Despite this, he is one of the rare people who really seems to get it when it comes to the complications and stresses that parenting can cause between spouses. One day while having breakfast with Ben, I began mildly complaining about my husband. Okay, maybe it was more like a tirade or bitchy venting session. I was detailing the number of things I was doing to get ready for the holidays. I explained how Kevin had been doing nothing and then he had the audacity to question the gift I had gotten for his mother! I complained to Ben that I worked as many hours as Kevin did and I always got stuck doing all the extra tasks while he just took for granted the fact that it would be taken care of, and... well, you get the point.

Ben said, "Wait a minute, why are you doing things for *his* family?" So I explained how I was the better shopper and event planner so it made sense for me to do it. I told him how, once you have kids, the lines get blurred with regards to extended family, and how his family did a lot for us. Then I told him one of life's unfair truths: gift giving and other thoughtful acts of kindness (like remembering birthdays) really reflect on the woman or primary caregiver in the relationship, wrongly or rightly. So that was why I had to take care of it myself. Ben replied, "Too bad. He is a grown man. He should be in charge of all things that relate to *his* family. That is his job; they are *his* family." I was speechless. I can honestly say that in the ten years I had been married to my husband I had never, ever once even considered asking him to handle anything like that for his family. I consider myself to be an assertive, highly verbal woman who does not have issues talking about what is fair and unfair. Yet I had never questioned this seemingly pre-determined role. It was almost comical.

Later that evening, I asked Kevin if he would please take over selecting the gifts he would like to give his mother, step-mother, father, sisters and grandmothers for the holidays. While on the subject, I added a request for him to please get in the habit of calling them back when they tried to reach him, instead of me being the designated communicator. In most cases they really wanted to talk their son or brother or grandson—not his wife anyway. He said, "Of course, sure, I can do that."

Think about it. How could someone say *no* to doing things for *their own family*? I was impressed at how easy that whole exchange was.

Ah, Not So Fast.....

The first holiday season that Kevin was in charge of gifts for his own family, I made a commitment to remind him only once. Then I broke out in a rash trying *not* to butt-in while he waited until the last minute, incurring overnight shipping charges. He forgot to buy cards, got the sizes wrong, forgot a few people entirely and generally worked himself (and me) into a panic. But I managed to remain steadfast in my commitment, keeping Ben's words in my mind. And of course, I still had plenty to do myself.

The hard part in asking someone for help is actually letting them help you without a) taking the project back or b) micro-managing the other person, causing them to hate helping you or c) telling them what a bad job they are doing and how you would have done it differently. Over the years my husband has improved greatly at his holiday tasks, and it is astounding to me that I was working so hard to pull off Christmas all by myself for all of those years. No wonder I was bitter! The benefits go beyond creating a fair distribution of labor. I think it makes him feel good about himself, and it definitely makes me feel good about him. Now, when I have a suggestion or even occasionally take care of something on his list for him, he appreciates that I am doing the job *for* him rather than taking my help for granted. And that makes all the difference in the world in our relationship.

Ideas And Potential Solutions

1. *Ask for help*

Over the next week, ponder the division of labor in your home. If things are very askew (and they usually are) consider *politely* asking your spouse to take on a few additional things. Just asking your partner to make school lunches or take over meal planning on two days of the week can be life changing in most households. Go back over the list and review the items you starred, and checkmark the items that could be farmed out to hired help or could be incorporated into your partner's world. In many cases, women tell me that their partners have been suggesting ideas to lighten their loads for years but they were too stressed and overwhelmed to know what to give up. Perhaps your partner can take over birthday party planning if your children are older. They usually know what they want, and as a family, you can all agree on a date and a budget. Hand over control and see what happens. Maybe your kids need to begin to make their own beds or do their own laundry. (Yes, you will have to teach them, and yes, they will do it wrong and might ruin something). Or maybe your family needs to hire a lawn service. If you catch yourself saying, "Oh, it's just easier to do it myself," just remember that while this may be true in the short run, it certainly is not true in the long run. And that is exactly the kind of thinking that got you where you are to begin with. Start small, but let some things go. And once you decide to let go, let go.

2. *Hire some help*

Of course, if hired help were the secret to a happy marriage and a harmonious home, then Hollywood would have a lower divorce rate. Hiring help is not the only answer, and it will certainly not solve all of your problems. But keeping things the same is not a good idea if you are carrying too much of the burden *and* you truly feel that your partner cannot take on one more thing. You might need some outside help, and it might be cheaper and easier than you think.

> *You can't wring your hands and roll up your sleeves at the same time.*
>
> *-US Senator Pat Schroeder*

But I Cannot Afford To Hire Help!

If you need help, get creative. You would be surprised how reasonably priced help can be when compared to the impact it can have on our lives. Like many Americans, my family and I have hired house sitters to care for our dogs, fish, plants, etc., while we were away. We have always been really careful to choose only the most responsible house sitters because so much can happen to a home during a week away. Some years ago I got the idea to ask our house sitter if she wanted to do some projects while she was in our home to earn extra money. She said, "Absolutely."

When I asked her what kinds of things she liked to do (since there was no end to the list of stuff that needed to be done in my home) she said she liked to organize and clean. Jackpot! Before our trip I went through the house and marked cupboards, closets and a few other things that she could work on while we were gone. We came home from our trip to find that four of our utility closets plus *all* of the kitchen cupboards had been cleaned, sanitized and organized beautifully. My junk drawers were organized within an inch of their lives. All of this for $125 more than it would have cost me *not* to have it done. I know, I know, an extra $125 doesn't grow on trees, but c'mon, if you could walk into your home today to find fifteen cupboards and closets cleaned and organized, what would you pay? And really, in my former life I had been known to spend more than that on a pair of sunglasses. The only thing better than taking a vacation is coming home from vacation to find that your chores have *progressed without you*.

Maybe your cupboards are already perfect. Here are some other random ideas to consider for lightening your burden in a meaningful and helpful way:

▶ Hire kids in the neighborhood (ages 8-14) for yard work, organization of the toy room or as a mother's helper to play with the kids while you get stuff done around the house. If you find someone good at a great rate, then pre-book him or her weekly. Believe me, you will find things for them to do.

▶ Ask your current childcare worker or housekeeper if they would like to earn a little more by doing a little more. If someone is already cleaning your home regularly, ask them how much more they would charge to do a couple loads of laundry or start a meal once per week. It can't hurt to ask.

▶ For meals, give some serious consideration to one of the meal prep places in your area. They usually have catchy names like *Dinner and Dish*. The basic premise is that you assemble 6-12 entrees at their store and take them home to freeze. You thaw an entrée in the fridge the day before you need it and then can usually cook it in a few easy steps. Even the total foodies (like me), who cook for therapy and love all things food, use this type of service. I am just too tired to think up what to cook during the week, and if I don't have something thawing, I will order out, which costs more and is usually less healthy. The concept is hard to get your head around initially, and many husbands will resist the idea at first (not sure why — that is a whole other Oprah Show!), but there is no denying that home-cooked meals save time and money over take-out.

▶ Get serious about trades and bartering. Many moms trade with other couples for childcare date nights. The concept of trading can go way beyond that. You can work with another parent to double the quantity you make for a few dinners in a row and then swap. Or perhaps you have a profession that lends itself well to trading services or goods, like masseuse, hairstylist, copy editor, etc. Bartering takes some effort and follow-through, but it can really pay off. (Check with your state laws and your CPA about how to book and claim barters and trades).

Things do not have to be split 50/50 between you and your partner for you to feel happy, even if you both work. You would be surprised how good it feels to be at 60/40 or even 70/30, depending upon how skewed your division of labor currently is.

Final Words On You Doing "Everything"

Regardless of your arrangement with your spouse in the income category, your *partner is a parent.* You cannot and should not try to "save" your partner from that role by doing *everything.* The moment you became a mother, your partner became a parent too. Raising kids is a major deal and relegating one person to the role is not sustainable for most people over the long run. It's just too much for one person and doing it all denies your partner the personal satisfaction of contributing to the well-being and raising of your children. With all due respect to how hard one must work to earn an income, being the breadwinner simply cannot be the *only* thing one partner does. Even Steven Spielberg runs carpool, makes dinners and volunteers for his kids sporting events (while making amazing movies) because he is a father.

> *Every marriage is its own little economy, a business of two with a finite number of resources that need to be allocated efficiently.*
> —*Paula Szuchman and Jenny Anderson,*
> *authors of Spouseanomics*

Ten ideas to make things easier for me:

1.
2.
3.
4.
5.
6.
7.
8.
9.
10.

Notes on Division of Labor: _____

_____

_____

_____

_____

_____

_____

_____

CHAPTER ELEVEN

ON THE RIGHT TRACK

"Dorothy, you've had the power all along."

-The Wizard Of OZ

The New "Mother-hood"

Becoming a mother healed the premature loss of my own mother and repaired my broken heart. In the blur of activity after my son's birth I can recall the pain mixed with the sense of accomplishment and confusion, and then something akin to a beam of light as the nurse put him in my arms. I felt like the Universe *was* generously compensating me for the earlier loss I'd endured by handing me 8.4 pounds of perfection. At that very moment I was struck with the realization that becoming a mother is largely about the honor of being entrusted with the complete responsibility of another person, whether we are ready or not. Simultaneously it occurred to me that it would not have mattered if I had adopted him, found him on a doorstep or grown him on my window sill --motherhood was epic regardless of whether it was science, mishap or miracle that had gotten me there.

While we all share a common bond and belong to the same mother tribe it's important to remember that motherhood is completely the same and yet completely different for each of us. While I felt a moment of total healing, another mother under similar circumstances might have felt grief or been overwhelmed by feelings of disconnection, depression or resentment toward the being who already needed so much (and ruined that girlish figure). Mothers of more than one child will attest to how dramatically different each birth experience and reaction can be.

Motherhood is a very big deal—even if your brother-in-law loves to remind you that, "Women have been doing it for millions of years!" And it can be a big deal in a completely different way for each of us.

As you move in the direction of cobbling together your own career and motherhood clarity remembering the similar-but-different concept can help you support other moms who make different choices than yourself. But much more importantly, it can help you make your own choices without the pressure to be the same. Even moms in the very same career lane likely made that choice for a different reason. Now you can look around at other lane choices and actually glean information that may assist you in your own decisions rather than having it reinforce what you do *not* want.

At the beginning of this book I asked you how your life would be different if you felt great about both your financial contribution (whatever that may be) and your job of raising kids. For some of you the lights went on and you knew what to tweak, change and insist upon. For others this book was the first time you'd considered some of the concepts and you are pondering your next moves.

Hopefully you are a little clearer now about what beliefs and life experiences have impacted your decisions and if you want those beliefs and experiences playing a big role in future decisions ....or not so much. And hopefully your ears perk up now when you hear someone pedaling the usual maternal folklore about money, parenting, "simplicity" and happiness. Now you apply your own logic and real-life-math and not let the person make you feel guilty or conflicted about your choices.

In my perfect world you have also noticed your judgments about other moms and can see where your own stress impacts your judgments. Does it make a little more sense now why only you (and your mate) can figure out the best set-up for *your* family and why there is not one, *RIGHT* career lane for all moms? No one else can truly understand how you got to this very place in your life or what *you* hold to be the most valuable and sacred elements of your parenting. Similarly there is no way that your beliefs could realistically apply to everyone else. My hope is that this book allowed you to quiet the outer noise of "shoulds" and "coulds" and "ought-tos" and clear the way to discovering what the best lane for you might be, even though you know that none of the lanes are easy or simple or *ideal*. Now you realize that each lane comes with its very own set of pros and cons in spite of the positive or negative hype that lane might get.

Perhaps when you feel really, really mad about something you'll remember to "go to the ugly" and see what other thoughts and feelings might be there to help you move forward. Maybe you and your spouse sat down (with a pitcher of margaritas or pot of coffee) and really talked about who does what around the house and for a moment you felt supported and connected and could ask for what you really need and that conversation helped the two of you move forward. Perhaps you made a list of ideas and are just pondering and thinking about that list and your realizations about the lanes. Maybe you've simply noticed that your mind is giving you ideas that you never considered before.

People have starkly different reactions to the ideas in this book. Of course I see this as evidence of how different we are and affirmation of why we should not be telling each other which lane to choose. Many insightful and generous moms read this book before it was published to help me see if I was on the right track and I was amazed and delighted to hear the different realizations they had.

Here is a sampling of a few:

► "I had no idea how mad I really was about the division of labor in my home. Now I have some constructive ideas to discuss with my husband rather than just feeling angry all of the time."

► "I thought I wanted to be a stay-home mom and now I see that I so don't. I want to work part-time."

▶ "Working is one of most important decisions we make as parents. I truly want to be home with my kids and I am so glad to know this about myself before much more time passes."

▶ "I have always felt guilty for working. I felt like a horrible mom. Now I accept that I am a good mom and I just need to ask for more help and stop feeling guilty all the time."

▶ "I am going to be nicer to my husband. He does a lot more than I thought. Very eye opening."

▶ "I now go to the ugly with regularity. It's very helpful."

▶ "I was about to say yes to something the other day, like I always do, and I thought about your book and I said NO. It was liberating."

▶ "You are even more of a safety freak than I am! And that is saying something. If you can quiet your fears then I can too."

▶ "The stuff about the other mothers really hit home for me. I judge other mothers and not surprisingly I feel very judged."

▶ "As convenient as it is working from home, I need more social contact. I feel isolated and I can't believe it but I belong in an office."

How about you? What did you learn about yourself as you did the exercises and read about the various lanes? What did you learn about what you really want at this age and stage of your life career-wise? Why is this important to you?

For some of us the answers to these questions come easily and for some of us it's a longer process and the realizations come in bits and pieces. Know that if you have done the exercises in the book and allowed yourself some thoughtful moments of wondering then you *are* processing the information and you can be on the look-out for ideas and strategies that might work for you and your lane choice.

As a final exercise I would suggest you make a list of small actions you *are* willing to take to make your current lane **better** or outline your plan to change lanes entirely. My clients will attest that the smaller the actions the more likely you are to actually follow- through and that act of following-through leads to more and more positive action. If you are unsure go back and re-read all of your answers and see if the list comes from that action.

Whatever you decide to act upon or not act upon, be nice to my friend (that would be YOU) and let yourself dream a little about a life where you feel mostly satisfied with your choices — even on the bad days. Think about what you really want and figure out the "how" later. I love that old saying, "If Mama ain't happy, ain't nobody happy" because it's essentially true even if it's crude. If you are in the right lane according to your wiring and *your* preferences then it's highly likely that you can do your best parenting from that lane — in spite of the difficulties and obstacles each lane brings.

Down the road as your family grows and your circumstances change, and they will, new lanes might make more sense. You are now armed with the skills to help you put your blinkers on and change lanes with confidence as you ask yourself once again, *What's My Lane?*

NOTES:

ACKNOWLEDGEMENTS

I must first and foremost thank my remarkable husband Kevin. Not only did he let me talk about him in the book, he also listened to my never-ending reasons for wanting to write it and endured hearing about countless versions and variations of the manuscript. He and our son Noah are far and away the best things that have ever happened to me — truly. Thank you, my dudes. Next I have to thank Shelly Humbach. I met Shelly shortly after tragedy hit in my young life and she has been right there by my side ever since. She also had babies long before I did and I learned most of the things I know about parenting from her. Shelly coined the phrase, "How can something with such a little butt completely run our lives?" and truer words have never been spoken. Thanks Shell! Also near the tippity-top of my thank-you list is my friend, Mary LoVerde. When I met Mary I had two books out and she had none. Then I fumbled, worked and procrastinated for more than ten years while she cranked out four amazing books, and I still hadn't finished this one. Her patience, encouragement, editing and coaching have been priceless. Thank you, Mary. I <u>literally</u> could not have done it without you.

Acknowledgements continued....

Thanks to my publishing coach, Robin Coffman (AKA The Manuscript Whisperer) and editors Dayna Dunbar and Marianne Brandon. Special thanks to Sam Horn (The famous Book Shepherd) for the book title, cover help and great writing advice. A partial list of my most involved readers must also be acknowledged: Kym Miller, Ashley Sakker, Margaret Pudyk, Christy Pudyk, Beth Conover, Dr. Carrie Merscham, Dr. Deb Freisen, Diana Golden, Leanne Iscaro, Jen LaFlam and Mary Anne Richmond. Thanks to those who helped with research and formatting including Wendy Hobbs, Peggy DePew, Nancy Schlechten, Emily Reynolds and Sarah Squires.

For the writing encouragement and editing for earlier versions of the manuscript I thank Mara Stets, Molly Cox Ziton, Elda Orr, Joy Hood, Mark LeBlanc, Louise Dunn, Matthew Stevens, Megan Tolomotu and Gail Crachiola.

ABOUT THE AUTHOR

Brenda is the President of Management Momentum LLC.
Management Momentum began when Brenda Abdilla discovered she was just as good at helping people reach their goals as she was at reaching and surpassing her own. Brenda has been helping professionals tackle tough business challenges, overcome crisis of confidence and navigate the career fast-track ever since.

Her mentoring approach is confidently different. Brenda possesses the leading credentials in the coaching profession strengthened by years of working with some of the best tools of the trade like the DiSC profile, Emotional Intelligence Quotient and the Enneagram. She uses this experience to create a custom, goal-oriented plan for each professional she mentors. Focus is placed on application of knowledge and outcomes versus simply telling a person what to do. The result is professional development that sticks with a person for the remainder of their career.

Brenda has used her multitude of talents for innumerable aspects over the years including author, speaker, sales superstar, recruiter and now professional mentor. Her ability to be direct, but kind has led to real, sustainable momentum for her clients.

Brenda's passions extend beyond the workplace. She is an advocate for community safety through The Watch House organization and creating a vibrant life with her husband and son in their Denver community. Visit Brenda's website to sign up for her free newsletter, The Coaching Minute, and to get an extra copy of some of the exercises in this book. www.ManagementMomentum.net

CPSIA information can be obtained at www.ICGtesting.com
Printed in the USA
LVOW11s1619150414

381823LV00008B/149/P

9 781481 904513